COIN
COLLECTORS'
HANDBOOK

REVISED EDITION

By
FRED REINFELD
Revised by Beatrice Reinfeld

DOUBLEDAY & COMPANY, INC.

GARDEN CITY, NEW YORK

OTHER BOOKS OF INTEREST

CJ 1830
R4
1976 X
copy 2

ACKNOWLEDGMENTS

In compiling the values of coins for this volume, careful study has been devoted to published authorities, as well as prices quoted in recent dealer advertisements and auction sales.

In particular, the book owes a great deal to the cordial cooperation of Burton Hobson.

The magnificent enlarged photographs which appear on pages 14-21 were made by DeVere Baker of the American Numismatic Society. The coins illustrating the various conditions were selected by the Capitol Coin Company.

Revised Edition
Copyright © 1976, 1971, 1970, 1969, 1967, 1966, 1965, 1963,
1962, 1961, 1960, 1959, 1958, 1956, 1954
by Sterling Publishing Co., Inc.
419 Park Avenue South, New York, N.Y. 10016
Manufactured in the United States of America
All rights reserved
Library of Congress Catalog Card No.: 62–18628
ISBN 0–385–11410–9

CONTENTS

Aetna, silver tetradrachm (465 B.C.). A magnificent ancient coin of unsurpassed workmanship.

Danzig, silver necessity taler (1577). One of the finest of all numismatic portraits of Christ.

Tyre, silver tetradrachm (about 125 B.C.-100 A.D.). This coin is thought to be the one used to pay Judas for his betrayal.

This bronze coin, thought to have been issued by Pontius Pilate (about 30 A.D.) may be the "widow's mite" mentioned in the New Testament.

United States, Washington cent (1791). A pre-Mint coin issued to honor our first President.

Roman Empire, bronze as (154-155 A.D.). The figure of Britannia was to appear on many British coins centuries later.

I. WHY COIN COLLECTING IS FASCINATING

Besides coin collectors, there are all kinds of collectors. Some people collect stamps or works of art. Others find stones, ship models, clocks, dolls, or old maps irresistible. Some are absorbed in buttons; others treasure old-time phonograph recordings, while others cherish snakes.

We may raise our eyebrows at the man who gives all his spare time to collecting beetles; but we may be sure that he prizes his treasures just as keenly as we prize our coins. Yet, of all the different kinds of collecting hobbies, coin collecting has a special attraction of its own.

Coins are miniature works of art. They are beautiful to look at, and many a collector has given a lifetime to repeatedly studying his favorite coins.

There is an added pleasure, of course, in possessing coins that are hard to get. These are not always necessarily expensive, for they sometimes turn up by chance in the most unexpected places—in the proverbial attic or occasionally in an otherwise almost worthless heap of ordinary coins. And, surprising as it may seem, quite valuable coins are found in ordinary change.

The fact that coins are made of metal, and are therefore *durable,* greatly increases their attractiveness. This durability relates them to the past and to the future as well. Since coins can last for thousands of years, they can be stored away and held for future profit. Most of this book will deal with coin values, but first let's consider coins as souvenirs of bygone times.

There are hundreds of types of Greek and Roman coins that are 2,000 years old—and more. Some of these Greek coins are so breathtakingly beautiful that you will find them regarded among the choicest art masterpieces of ancient Greece. The Roman coins are remarkable for the unflattering frankness of the portraits of the Emperors.

Greek coins are comparatively rare and therefore apt to be expensive. Of Roman coins the opposite is true. Remember that the Roman Empire was widespread; it had a great deal of coinage over a period of centuries in large areas of Europe, Africa, and Asia. Hoards of Roman coins are still being dug up.

Coins as witnesses of the past

Every coin tells us something about the history of the period when it was minted. There are coins from Biblical times, and others that remind us of the victorious campaigns of Alexander the Great—one of the outstanding military leaders of all time.

Coming to times nearer our own, the artistic glory of the Renaissance is mirrored on coins just as excitingly as the ideals and upheavals of the French Revolution. In the United States, the struggle of the Colonies to achieve independence has been represented on some of our most beautiful coins. Similarly, the tragic and bitterly-fought War Between the States has inspired some of the most distinguished coins.

There are many British coins with fascinating historical associations: the Tudor rose on Henry VII's beautiful gold sovereign (1489), the Puritan Revolution coinage, the famous "gun money" of James II, and the familiar figure of Britannia.

Left: Thrace (323-281 B.C.), head of Alexander the Great. *Center:* U.S., Liberty Bell. *Right:* Scales of justice, from a coin issued during the French Revolution.

The famous pieces of eight coined by the Spanish government in Mexico call to mind the colorful treasure galleons of the Silver Fleet, as well as the brutality and daring of the Conquistadores who enslaved the Indians to get that treasure. Despite all the debunking of intriguing tales of hoards buried by pirates, there are those who still hope to find fortunes on some sun-drenched beach.

Alexander the Great and Napoleon are by no means the only famous men who appear on coins. Julius Caesar issued coinage to glorify himself. Simon Bolívar, the liberator of South America, has been honored by several countries. Oliver Cromwell, Frederick the Great, and Gustavus Adolphus of Sweden are some of the other commanders whose likenesses were struck on coins.

United States coinage has for the most part used impersonal themes suggesting liberty. (Interestingly enough, our favorite device, the eagle, goes back to Greek and Roman models.) George Washington, Abraham Lincoln, Thomas Jefferson, Benjamin Franklin, and Franklin D. Roosevelt are the only men who have appeared on our regular coinage. The Lincoln Head cent was the first of our regular coins to carry a portrait, and it was not issued until 1909.

As far as coinage is concerned, this is mostly a man's world. Nevertheless, some famous women have appeared on coins. Maria

Left: One of the many coins Napoleon Bonaparte issued with his likeness. *Right:* Maria Theresa taler, issued into the 20th century with the same date—1780.

Left: A handsome coin of Athens (about 150 B.C.) picturing the goddess Athene (Minerva). *Right:* another religious coin, picturing a Hebrew temple. The coin was issued in 132-135 A.D. during the second Jewish revolt against the Romans.

Theresa, Empress of Austria, first appeared on a taler of 1780 which became one of the most famous coins ever issued. Used extensively in trade with Africa and the Levant, this coin was issued for many years—always with the original date, regardless of the actual year of issue.

Religious themes have been used surprisingly often on coinage. The ancient Greeks and Romans, for example, pictured their gods and goddesses on their coins.

The coinage of the Holy Land during Biblical times has fascinated many collectors. A number of handsome and nowadays rare coins appeared. Among the Jewish coins was one of a temple with the Ark of the Covenant.

Many numismatic scholars have tried to trace the original "tribute penny" about which Jesus advised, "Render unto Caesar the things that are Caesar's and unto God the things that are God's." The most popular theory is that the "tribute penny" was a coin of Tiberius, the Emperor who reigned from 14 to 37 A.D.

The "widow's mite" was obviously a coin of a small denomination, and the difficulty here is that there were a number of such coins in Judea. A bronze coin that may have been struck by Pontius Pilate is one of the leading candidates for the honor of "widow's mite."

Another subject for keen speculation is the identity of the thirty pieces of silver received by Judas Iscariot for his betrayal. The tetradrachm issued by the Phoenician city of Tyre is considered the most likely "piece of silver."

Representations of Christ appear on later coins of a number of countries. One of the most impressive is a taler issued by the "free city" of Danzig during a siege in 1577.

The largest amount of religious coinage is of course that of the

One of the most beautiful Papal coins, and in fact one of the most striking coins ever issued. It appeared during the Papacy of Alexander VII (1655-166*l*).

Popes. Many of the Papal coins are notable for their handsome appearance and distinguished workmanship.

One American coin is interesting from the religious viewpoint —the two-cent piece first issued in 1864 (page 52). This was the first coin to bear the motto, "In God We Trust."

The intrinsic value of coins

The fact that coins are made of metal is one of the things that sets off coin collecting from other collecting hobbies. The metal in the coin is worth something. When the metal in question is gold or silver, the value may be substantial.

This makes coins a good investment. In times of inflation the value of a coin rises considerably; at all other times its worth as mere metal establishes a floor below which the value of the coin cannot fall.

The interchangeability of coins as coins, and coins as metal, has created problems ever since coinage started. For hundreds of years the crimes of "shaving" and "clipping" coins were so prevalent in England that culprits met with the drastic penalty of having their right hands chopped off.

The United States coinage revision law of 1853 illustrates what happens when a government changes the content of coins. In this case the law slightly reduced the content of several silver denominations. This led to a great deal of melting down of pre-1853 coins, because *those* coins were then worth more as silver bullion than they were as coins. The ultimate result—a very interesting one to coin collectors—has been a scarcity of certain types of silver coins issued before 1853.

One of the most vexing problems relating to the value of a

coin's content is the question of alloys. These are cheap or "base" metals blended with a more costly or "precious" metal.

The legitimate reason for using alloys is that a small amount of tin, copper, or zinc will make a coin able to withstand a lot of wear and thus keep it in circulation for a much longer time. Gold can be hammered or beaten to a thinness of 1/365,000th of an inch. This is a great asset for metalworking, but it can be a serious drawback when gold is used in coins. The addition of a small amount of alloy gives us a much sturdier coin.

The same holds true for silver coins. In the United States, until 1965, these were generally 900 fine—that is, 900 grains of silver to 100 grains of alloy. "Clad" dimes and quarters with an outer layer of copper-nickel (75% copper, 25% nickel) bonded to an inner core of pure copper came into use in 1965. The silver content of the half dollar was reduced to 40% in the same year, to be eliminated completely in favor of "clad" coins in 1971. By 1947 the "silver" coinage of England lost all its silver content, being replaced by coins that were 75 per cent copper and 25 per cent nickel.

In the past such changes, known as "debasing," have played havoc with a country's coinage. One of the worst "debasing" policies of relatively modern times was carried out by Henry VIII, to the point where his silver coins were one-third silver and two-thirds copper. This miserable coin, issued in 1544, earned him the name of "Old Coppernose." But even this debasing was mild compared to what happened to the coinage of the Roman Empire. Over a period of centuries the coinage deteriorated from a fine silver content to almost complete alloy with a shallow wash of silver over it.

This is the silver shilling, issued in 1544, that gave Henry VIII of England the contemptuous nickname of "Old Coppernose." The coin is one of the worst examples of debasing in relatively recent times.

Changes in U.S. coins were also made before. This happened to our coinage of cents and nickels in World War II. In 1943 copper was needed so badly for wartime use that steel—a more valuable metal—was substituted in the cents issued that year. (The change worked out badly, however, as it resulted in confusion between the steel cent and the silver dime.)

The other change of metal content took place in the nickel. From 1942 to 1945 all nickel disappeared from this coin because of wartime demand. Silver, intrinsically more valuable, replaced the usual nickel content. Thus for four years the "nickel" had no nickel.

Hoards and finds

We often hear of jars and pots full of valuable coins being dug up by accident. Sometimes these treasures come to light when daring youngsters venture into an abandoned house; sometimes the proverbial tin box turns up in a cellar or attic that needs repairing. In Europe and parts of Africa and Asia the discovery of ancient Greek and Roman hoards has been an everyday occurrence for centuries.

A kettle buried under a woodpile; glass jars hidden in an old barn; a metal container sealed in a tile wall; a box concealed behind a partition—why were these treasures hoarded away in the first place?

Since ancient times, hoarding has often been stimulated by wars, invasions, sieges, inflations, famines. The formation of great banking systems made slow inroads on this "squirrel" psychology. In fairly recent times, people living in outlying areas, far from a bank, preferred to hide their money in what they considered a safe place. Even when a bank was easily accessible, they were distrustful and still insisted on keeping their treasures nearby.

And so from time to time we read stories of unexpected finds of hidden money. These stories provide one of the fascinations of coin collecting. Every true collector feels that some day, somehow, luck will come his way and he will hit upon the find of a lifetime.

2. HOW TO DETERMINE A COIN'S CONDITION

Have you ever noticed how people react to the condition of coins? They take a childlike pleasure in a bright, clear, shiny, sharply outlined coin. Even if it's only a penny, they find something festive and cheerful about a coin when it's brand-new—just put into circulation.

On the other hand, a worn, faded, tired-looking coin, even if it's worth fifty times the value of a shiny penny, evokes no emotional reaction at all. We part with it readily, whereas disposing of the shiny new penny costs us something of a pang.

Well, the man who feels that slight tinge of regret is really akin to the coin collector, who loves coins for their own sake. The physical state of coins—*their condition*—is tremendously important to the collector. A coin in splendid condition is a desirable coin—a miniature work of art. It is likely to be worth considerably more than its face value. But a worn, faded coin is depressingly close to an anonymous metal disc, totally lacking in distinctive character.

Coin conditions

Since there is a price tag on the different kinds of conditions, it is important for the collector to be familiar with the gradations of condition. Both in buying and selling, the description of the coin's condition must be clear and accurate.

Uncirculated (Unc.): In new condition. All lettering, the date and details of the design are extremely clear. In the modern minting process, coins slide down chutes and are packed and shipped loose in bags. Even an uncirculated coin may show a few light scratches, or abrasions, or scuff marks from this rough handling. An uncirculated coin, however, shows no sign of wear or serious damage at any point. An absolutely perfect coin is often described as Gem

Uncirculated or FDC (Fleur de Coin). Uncirculated coins are often brilliant but not necessarily so.

Extremely Fine (Ef or XF): Similar to Uncirculated except that the very highest points of the design show the slightest signs of wear or rubbing. All fine detail is still clear and coins in this condition may even have a little mint luster left.

Very Fine (VF): Design still quite clear; however, the coin begins to show definite signs of wear. The lettering may be worn but the complete outline of every letter is still clear. The highest points of the design show smooth spots of wear.

Fine (F): A considerably worn but still desirable coin. The basic outline is still clear but much of the fine detail is lost. Portions of some of the lettering may be worn away.

Very Good (VG): A much worn but not altogether unattractive coin. A coin in this condition should be free of serious gouges or other mutilations but it may be somewhat scratched from use.

Good (G): A really minimum condition coin. The date and mint mark would be legible and major portions of the design distinguishable.

Fair: Coins in fair condition are usually not acceptable to collectors. They may have only partial dates, be dark in color and parts of the design may be completely worn away. They are generally used as "space fillers" only until such time as a better coin can be had.

Poor: Coins in poor condition are usually highly undesirable. They may be bent, corroded and completely worn down.

Proof sets

Proof coins are specially prepared with the finest workmanship and materials that modern technique can devise. They are the choicest of all our coins, as far as condition is concerned. This makes them highly desirable coins, as far as most collectors are concerned. How this bears on the value of proof coins is described on page 31 and page 34.

The subject of coin condition is far from academic. As you will see in later chapters, condition is one of the crucial factors that determines a coin's value and suitability for investment.

Now look at these coins (in their exact size) side by side and notice the variation.

In order to describe in detail just how these generalized terms apply to an actual coin, let's examine greatly enlarged photographs of the reverses of eight Liberty Head ("Barber") Quarters.

Uncirculated

All the details are sharply outlined:

the shield	the eagle's claws
the eagle's eye	the arrows
the eagle's neck	the leaves
the eagle's feathers	the dots in the border

the dots between "United" and "Quarter" and between "America" and "Dollar"
the lettering on the inscription
the lettering on the ribbon

Extremely Fine

All the details are still distinct.

Note, however, that there are slight scratches on the shield, and that the feathers are slightly faded toward the sides.

There is no proof coin in these photographs, for the high luster of a proof does not show up well in a photo. In evaluating the various conditions, we shall consider 11 features of the reverse of these coins.

Very Fine

The eagle's eye and neck are distinct, and so are the arrows, the leaves, the dots and lettering on the inscription.

The shield is fairly distinct, but there are some nicks on it, and there are traces of fading toward the sides.

The feathers are considerably faded toward the sides, and the outside dots are beginning to grow fuzzy.

The claws are still fairly distinct, and so is the lettering on the ribbon, although *unum* is a little faded.

Fine

The shield and the eagle's eye are fairly distinct. However, there are some nicks and scratches on the shield and the fading toward the edges is getting more pronounced.

The neck is considerably faded, and the feathers are badly faded toward the sides.

The arrows, the leaves, and the lettering on the inscription are still distinct, and the dots in the inscription can be clearly seen.

The dots in the border have become fuzzier than in the previous condition.

The lettering on the ribbon is faded somewhat and several letters are unreadable.

The claws are no longer as distinct as they were previously.
(Note the "D" mint mark under the eagle.)

Very Good

The eagle's eye, the leaves, the dots and the lettering on the inscription are still distinct.

The lines on the shield are completely gone, and the details on the neck have almost disappeared.

Little of the detail on the feathers is left, and the claws seem to merge with the arrows and leaves.

The arrows have grown fuzzy, and the dots in the border are no longer distinct.

The lettering on the ribbon is badly faded and is becoming more unreadable.

Good

The shield is completely faded; all detail is gone on the neck.

The leaves, the inscription dots, and the inscription lettering are still distinct.

The eye is rather faint, the feathers are almost completely faded, and the claws are no longer sharply outlined.

The arrows are becoming fuzzy, and the dots in the border are considerably faded.

Most of the lettering on the ribbon is unreadable.

Fair

General comment: badly scratched and blotched.

The leaves are still distinct—the only good feature.

One of the inscription dots is clear, the other faded.

The inscription lettering is decidedly weaker than previously; the ribbon lettering is completely unreadable.

The claws are no longer sharply outlined, and the remaining features are completely rubbed off.

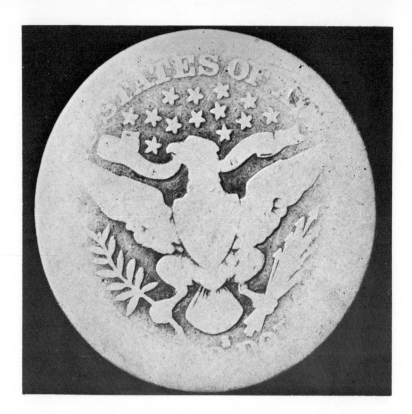

Poor

The leaves are still fairly distinct, but all the other details are completely or almost completely rubbed off.

3. HOW TO TAKE CARE OF COINS

Taking proper care of your coins will greatly increase your pleasure in collecting. By the same token, careless treatment of your coins may prove inconvenient or costly in the long run.

Certain basic problems arise for every collector: How should you handle coins? What is the best way to store them? Is cleaning advisable, or will it damage coins? How do you detect counterfeit coins?

Let's consider these problems.

Handling coins

As we will see, coin condition has a direct relation to monetary value. A brilliant proof or uncirculated coin is not only more attractive than one that is worn and faded, but collectors will often pay a substantial premium for it. A coin that is valued at $2.50 in "good" condition may be worth $25.00 in uncirculated condition. Sometimes the spread is even greater.

How a collector handles his coins will therefore affect their appearance and their premium value. Here are a few useful rules to remember:

1. Always hold a coin by its edge. Holding the coin by its surface will bring it into contact with a certain amount of perspiration on your hand. Doing this repeatedly will undoubtedly result in a fading of the original sharpness of outline.

2. Don't keep coins in a bag or container where scratching and rubbing are bound to spoil the condition of the coins.

3. Don't drop or tap coins to hear the "ring" of the metal.

In storing your coins, give thought to the problem of how to protect them against tarnish.

Most collectors keep their coins in cabinets, albums, folders, or holders. Whatever method you choose, be sure your coins are free from any material that might be injurious to them. Your collection ought to be arranged in such a way that you can find a particular coin without spending a lot of time on the search.

Cabinets and trays

Some collectors like to keep their coins in cabinets made up of long trays. Such cabinets generally hold anywhere from 1,000 to 4,000 coins, depending on the size of the cabinet and the coins.

The trays in these cabinets are generally about 12 inches long and wide enough to hold the standard 2x2 coin envelope. Coin cabinets come in wood or steel, and on grounds of durability, steel is preferable by far. (Another point to remember is that certain woods—oak, for example—are very injurious to silver coins.)

The steel cabinets are made of electrically welded or cold rolled steel. A sliding backrest in each tray holds the coins in place when the tray is not completely filled. Coin envelopes, which are very moderately priced, are moisture proof and dust proof; they are made of kraft paper, glassine, or cellophane. The last two materials have the advantage of giving you a full view of obverse and reverse without your having to handle the coin itself.

Here is an interesting method of guarding against tarnish and at the same time providing an admirable filing system. After placing your coin in a transparent envelope, fold over the top quarter of an inch. Write or type all relevant information about the coin—identification, condition, date, amount of purchase, etc. —on a 2x2 area of an ordinary index card. Cut out the 2x2 area and staple it to the folded top of the envelope. Then the whole unit can be kept in a tray.

You can improve on this system by using index cards of different colors to denote coin conditions. Having all information

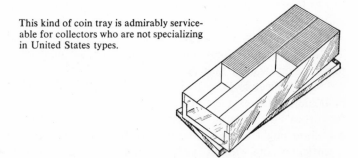

This kind of coin tray is admirably serviceable for collectors who are not specializing in United States types.

handy in this way will enable you to arrange your coins by country or type or subject. You will avoid exasperating delay in finding any particular coin you are looking for.

The cabinet and tray system is excellent if you are collecting the coins of a foreign country, or seventeenth-century talers, or ship coins, or some other specialized line which is off the beaten track. In fact, this system is a good one if you are not specializing at all, and merely acquiring whatever happens to strike your fancy.

Coin albums

However, if you are a type collector of United States coins, you will want some other method of arranging your collection. If you are assembling a set of Indian Head Cents or Jefferson Nickels, for example, you will find a coin album or coin holder or coin folder more suitable to your purpose.

The three methods differ as to cost, but they have certain features in common. They provide spaces cut to exact size for holding all or most of the coins of a given type. In many cases

(Above) Book-type coin albums combine the finest features for display and protection of your coins with ease of storage.

they take care of all the years a type was issued, and even offer space for coins with mint marks.

The albums come as ring binders for loose-leaf pages. It is possible to buy the appropriately printed cut-out pages for all the principal types of United States coins. There is a special set of pages, for example, for the Half Cents issued from 1793 to 1857; another set for all the Buffalo Nickels from 1913 to 1938; and so on. Pages for commemorative coins and proof sets are also available.

Each horizontal row of openings is protected by a movable section of transparent plastic which you can slide out when you want to insert a coin in that row. You then return the slide to its protective position. Once a coin is inserted in its proper place, it need never again be "touched by human hands." To look at the obverse or reverse, you need merely to turn the page.

The pages, which are made of sturdy cardboard with reinforced corners to withstand much use, come either printed or plain for the various sizes of coins. In the latter form, they enable you to make your own notations and arrangements.

Folders and holders

Coin albums are a highly satisfactory way of storing and displaying type collections, but they are fairly expensive. For the young collector who prefers a much more economical method, there are inexpensive cardboard coin folders which provide for about twenty different types of American coins. However, these show only one side of a coin, as you must press the coin into an opening cut exactly to size, and the back is pressed against cardboard.

When closed, these folders shut almost flat. The folders come printed or plain, and aside from those dealing with United States types, there are four Canadian folders. These have room for Large Cents, Small Cents, 5 Cents Silver, 5 Cents Nickel, and Dimes.

There are also many other kinds of coin holders which can be used for a variety of coins.

Among the most popular are lucite holders, made of transparent top and bottom plates. Some of these hold one coin, some a series. After the coins are fitted in snugly on the bottom plate,

Coin folders like this one enable collectors to keep coins of a series together in a convenient, economical format.

the top plate is securely fastened down with metal screws. In this way the coins show to best advantage; either side can be seen, and at the same time the coins are protected against tarnish. One such holder comes in almost thirty forms to provide for many of the most popular types of American coins.

Giant strides have been made in the last 20 years in improving coin-storing methods. The search for technical improvements is still going on, in order to give more satisfactory service to the collector.

Coin holders of lucite are among the most attractive means of displaying your highly-prized coins.

Cleaning coins

Coins, as we know, are extremely durable. Yet they are sooner or later affected by the passage of time, and this leads to the troublesome problem of whether or not they should be cleaned.

Copper or bronze eventually becomes filmed or encrusted with what is known as patina. Oxidation (the action of oxygen on the metal) changes the color of the coin to green, black, brown, red, or blue—or in some cases more than one of these colors. Patina is always present on ancient copper or bronze coins. What kind of color the coin takes on, depends on chemical changes that in turn depend on the moisture in the atmosphere and the composition of the nearby soil.

Silver coins—like all silver objects—eventually tarnish. Since condition is such an important factor in coin value, every collector hates to have any deterioration in his choice proofs and brilliant uncirculated coins. There are several tarnish-removers and coin-cleaning materials on the market, but none of them can be recommended unconditionally.

We have all heard of coins being ruined by cleaning, and it is often impossible to know in advance what will come of such an attempt. The experts are themselves divided on the advisability of cleaning or not cleaning. And it is significant that even when they recommend cleaning, they disagree violently as to the proper method of cleaning.

This all adds up to a very confusing picture. The best advice on the subject of cleaning, therefore, seems to be: *don't do it.* But if you insist on cleaning, have it done by an expert.

Some collectors lacquer their silver coins, and it is true that this method will preserve the coins for decades from tarnishing. But here again skillful work is essential. If you have ever lacquered a piece of furniture, you know how careful you must be to get a perfectly even tone and avoid lumpy or spotted surfaces. Then again, other collectors may dislike the lacquered appearance —a point to remember when you want to dispose of the coins.

Here is a vivid example of one of the outstanding differences between a genuine coin and a counterfeit coin. On the good coin the corrugated outer edge (known as the "reeding") is even and distinct. On the counterfeit coin, the ridges are crooked and indistinct.

Detecting counterfeit coins

From time to time a collector has the disagreeable experience of coming across counterfeit coins. The experience is all the more disagreeable if he is taken in by such a coin. We cannot approach the expertness of the Federal Reserve Bank examiners who can spot counterfeits in a heap of coins merely by feel and by a casual glance. However, you should find the following advice from the United States Secret Service most helpful:

1. If you suspect a coin, drop it gently on a hard surface. Genuine coins have a bell-like ring. Most counterfeit coins sound dull.

2. Feel all coins. Most counterfeit coins feel greasy.

3. The corrugated outer edge of genuine coins is even and regular. The edge of counterfeit coins is uneven, crooked, or missing in spots.

4. Most counterfeit coins can be easily cut with a knife. Genuine coins are not easily cut.

4. WHAT COIN VALUES DEPEND ON

If you ask a non-collector his opinion of what makes a coin valuable, he will answer unhesitatingly, "Rarity!" It is true that rarity is a large part of the answer, but it is not the whole answer.

Again in the eyes of a non-collector, the age of a coin is also a prime factor in determining value. This is true to some extent, but again it is not the whole story. The coin trade has other standards besides age and rarity in assessing coin values.

Supply and demand

The number of collectors of United States coins has been growing steadily for years. Thus, the demand for these coins is great, while the supply is more or less fixed, and this constantly pushes up the premium values of American coins.

Just as strong demand has a potent effect in raising prices, so does lack of demand leave prices on a fairly even keel. We have a good example of this in the field of ancient coins. The supply of these coins is limited, to be sure. But the *demand* for them is by no means as keen as the demand for American coins. That is why it is quite conceivable that an American coin may sell for several times the price of an ancient coin which is much scarcer.

While collectors admire handsome coins and are fascinated by their historical associations, these factors likewise play a small part in measuring "demand" and in determining coin values. One of the most beautiful coins of all time is the one coined by Lysimachus of Thrace with the portrait of Alexander the Great. Famous as this much-admired coin is, its price in "very fine" condition is about $50.00. This is less than the price of many an American coin which is available in much larger quantities in very fine condition.

Condition

As we have seen in Chapter 2, there is considerable variation in the physical state of coins—their condition. Collectors set great store by condition. They like to obtain a coin in the finest possible state they can afford.

Because this attitude is universal among collectors, condition plays a very important part in determining the premium value of a coin. The 1892 dime (from the Philadelphia mint) is a typical example, as the following values indicate:

Good	$1.75
Fine	5.50
Very Fine	8.00
Extremely Fine	14.00
Uncirculated	65.00
Proof	200.00

Mint marks

Mint marks are extremely important when we are determining the value of a coin. These marks are small letters struck on a coin to indicate the mint that issued it. At one time or another the United States has had seven mints, three of which are still in operation:

Mint		Mint Mark
Philadelphia, Pa.	1792 to date	none
Dahlonega, Ga.	1838-1861	D
Charlotte, N. C.	1838-1861	C
New Orleans, La.	1838-1909	O
San Francisco, Cal.	1854-1955; 1968-	S
Carson City, Nev.	1870-1893	CC
Denver, Colo.	1906 to date	D

(There is one exception to the rule that coins of the Philadelphia mint have never had mint marks. The wartime Jefferson Nickels of this mint had a P mint mark.)

Here is why mint marks are important: when a coin is issued by two or more mints in the same year, there may be a considerable difference in the quantities issued by each mint. Where there is a great variation in the number of coins issued, it is very likely that there will be a sizable difference in price.

The serious collector therefore finds it useful to be familiar with the quantities issued year by year, as shown in the annual mint reports. The case of the 1913 quarters is very instructive.

As you can see from the table below, there are sharp differences in the number of quarters issued by the three mints that year. Here are the values of the 1913 quarters in "uncirculated" condition:

Quantity	Mint	Mint Mark	Value
484,613	Philadelphia	none	$385.00
1,450,800	Denver	D	185.00
40,000	San Francisco	S	1,800.00

Thus the mint reports are in *most* cases a useful guide to values; but not in all cases. The early mint reports are sometimes unreliable, and in one famous case they have given rise to what has been rightly called the greatest mystery of American coinage.

According to the mint records 19,570 silver dollars were struck in 1804, yet only thirteen 1804 dollars are known today. Years of intensive research have failed to account for this startling discrepancy.

In some cases we know why the mint records of a given year do not tell the whole story. Sometimes the number of coins *struck* exceeded the number of coins *issued*. In such instances the extra coins may have been melted down, in some cases they may have been restruck with the date of the following year. In any event, it is only the early mint reports that occasionally prove unreliable.

5. COINS FOR INVESTMENT

To many collectors coins are a hobby, and a very enjoyable one. Others are interested in coins not only as a hobby but also as a form of investment.

From the investment point of view, American coins are much more desirable than foreign coins. The values of United States coins have been rising steadily for a good many years. As far as we can foresee at the present time, this trend will continue. The supply of coins is limited, while the number of collectors increases steadily.

With demand increasing from year to year, a collector has a reasonable—though not infallible—assurance that the United States coins he buys will rise substantially in value in the years to come.

Foreign coins also have increased substantially in value in recent years, but most collectors still prefer the coins of their own country.

How and where to buy

Buying depends on several factors. One is the collector's pocketbook. If his funds are strictly limited, he may have to confine his buying to the least expensive types. He may have to be satisfied with the "good" and "very good" conditions, rather than the "uncirculated" and "proof."

Buying also depends on the very nature of the individual collection. If it is of a fairly general kind, with no emphasis on a particular specialty, the collector can be guided by moderate prices, attractive designs, interesting historical features.

The collector of "types" has a fairly clear path before him— to fill in the gaps in a given series. In every type there are several years or mint marks that are scarce and relatively expensive. These will always be in great demand, for their absence leaves a set incomplete. This reasoning is not only logical, it is also costly.

The rarer the missing coin, the more desirable it becomes. The more desirable it becomes, the higher its value to you will be!

On the basis of past experience a collector is likely to develop a part-business, part-friendly association with several dealers on whom he will come to rely for the bulk of his purchases. In turn, these dealers, being familiar with his specialty, will cater more efficiently to his interests.

Practices of the coin trade

When we talk about the values of coins and the steady rise in values, we have to be very clear about what we mean by "value."

As used in this book and as generally understood among coin collectors and dealers, "value" means the price you are likely to have to pay for a given coin when you buy it from a dealer. *It does not mean the amount you can expect to realize if you want to sell the coin to a dealer.*

The dealer's *buying* price averages around half of his *selling* price. This is understandable, since his selling price has to include his cost of doing business plus a reasonable profit.

A small firm cannot afford to keep a great deal of money tied up in its stock of coins. Consequently its purchases from an individual have to be resold to a larger dealer and the cost of handling must necessarily be allowed for in setting the purchase price. A large firm, on the other hand, keeps an extensive inventory— a costly burden which can tie up considerable sums of money. This, too, places a limitation on the amount the larger dealer feels justified in paying for the coins he buys.

Still another motive influences the dealer. When presented with the opportunity to buy a small or miscellaneous collection, his general experience is that it contains a few highly desirable coins that he can resell very quickly. However, the bulk of the collection will be items that will probably move slowly. And so what the dealer really does is pay for the coins he can dispose of readily; the rest of the collection must come as part of the "package."

Selling at auction is recommended by some authorities. This type of sale is suitable, however, only for the disposal of collections which are quite large and contain a great many highly desirable items.

Trading with other collectors

As you've seen, a dealer's buying prices must necessarily be lower than his selling prices if he is to cover his overhead and other expenses and make a reasonable profit. Consequently, you may find you have a problem on your hands when you want to dispose of duplicates which are in less than exceptionally fine condition. Such coins, when fairly common, are merely a drug on the market as far as the dealer is concerned.

One of the best ways to dispose of such coins is doubtless through trading with other collectors. Sooner or later every collector acquires duplicates. When this happens to you, you naturally want to keep the coins which are in better condition and dispose of those in inferior condition. If you are on friendly terms with other collectors, the chances are you can arrange swaps.

However, a word of caution is necessary. Doing business with a well-established dealer will enable you to build up your collection satisfactorily, but dealings with strangers, or with people without proper references, may turn out badly.

So, while it may be possible to do a certain amount of business with other collectors, don't minimize the dealer's role! The bulk of a collector's transactions will always be with dealers, who render a service that cannot possibly be matched by collectors.

Making contacts with other collectors, it is true, can further your knowledge of numismatics. Anyone who has a favorite hobby is naturally interested in meeting others who share the same tastes. In comparing notes, collectors undoubtedly pick up many fine points about numismatics.

They further their knowledge in two different ways. In the first place, they can learn more about their own specialties from other collectors who have been in the field for a much longer time. And, on the other hand, they can acquire an interest in fascinating sidelines that have previously escaped their attention.

Thus, a collector who is interested in American Large Cents may strike up an acquaintance with a fellow collector who specializes in Irish Gun Money, or in current Canadian proof sets, or in nineteenth-century Latin American coinage, or in coinage of the Roman Empire. In every case the collector enlarges his interests and derives added enjoyment from his hobby.

6. CATALOG OF U. S. COINS

EARLY AMERICAN COINS

Among the coins which appeared before the first regular Mint issues of 1793, there is a great deal of variation, and considerable confusion or obscurity about their origin or the authority for issuing them.

CONTINENTAL DOLLAR

Year		Good	Fine
1776	Pewter; "CURENCY"	$400.00	$800.00
1776	Silver; "CURRENCY" (very rare)		
1776	Brass; "CURENCY" (rare)		
1776	Pewter; "CURRENCY"	400.00	850.00
1776	Pewter; E G FECIT	500.00	900.00
1776	Silver; E G FECIT (very rare)		

NOVA CONSTELLATIO COPPERS (CENTS)

Year		Good	Fine
1783	Pointed rays; "CONSTELLATIO"	22.50	60.00
1783	Blunt rays; "CONSTELATIO"	20.00	55.00
1785	Blunt rays; "CONSTELATIO"	25.00	60.00
1785	Pointed rays; "CONSTELLATIO"	15.00	45.00

BAR CENT

		Good	Fine
no date		200.00	400.00

Top left: the Continental Dollar, first issued in 1776. *Top right:* the Bar Cent, supposedly designed from Revolutionary soldiers' buttons, with 13 bars for the 13 states. *Bottom:* Nova Constellatio Cent, with 13 stars for the 13 states.

Most of the coins in this group were issued before the United States Mint began operating. President Washington on April 2, 1792 signed the bill authorizing the establishment of the Mint.

WASHINGTON PIECES

Year		Good	Fine	Unc.
1783	1 cent: draped bust on obverse; wreath on reverse	$15.00	$25.00	$125.00
1783	1 cent: draped bust on obverse; female figure on reverse	15.00	25.00	115.00
1783	1 cent: military bust on obverse; female figure on reverse	20.00	35.00	150.00
1783	1 cent: military busts on obverse and reverse ("double head cent"); no date	22.50	45.00	175.00
1791	1 cent: large eagle on reverse	45.00	95.00	425.00
1791	1 cent: small eagle on reverse	45.00	95.00	500.00
1791	"Liverpool" halfpenny	250.00	600.00	1500.00
1793	1 halfpenny; ship on reverse	50.00	75.00	300.00
1792	eagle cent, copper (rare)			
1792	eagle cent, silver (very rare)			
1792	eagle cent, gold (outstanding rarity)			
1792	1 cent: "WASHINGTON—PRESIDENT"	1200.00	2500.00	
1792	1 cent: "WASHINGTON—BORN VIRGINIA"	700.00	1500.00	
1792	half dollar, silver (rare)	1500.00	3000.00	
1792	half dollar, copper	500.00	1000.00	
1792	half dollar: large eagle on reverse (outstanding rarity)			
1795	1 cent: grate reverse	40.00	85.00	200.00
1795	1 cent: no date, LIBERTY AND SECURITY	50.00	100.00	350.00
1795	1 cent: date on reverse (rare)			
1795	halfpenny; lettered edge	17.50	150.00	100.00

FUGIO CENTS

Year		Good	Fine	Unc.
1787	1 cent ("STATES UNITED")	35.00	75.00	250.00
1787	1 cent ("UNITED STATES")	45.00	85.00	300.00
1787	1 cent: blunt rays	50.00	125.00	500.00
1787	1 cent ("UNITED" above, "STATES" below); rare			

There are some other varieties, generally quite rare.

EARLY MINT ISSUES

Year		Good	Fine
1792	half disme, silver	750.00	1250.00
1792	half disme, copper (outstanding rarity)		
1792	disme, silver (outstanding rarity)		
1792	disme, copper		
1792	1 cent; silver center (rare)		
1792	1 cent; no silver center (rare)		
1792	BIRCH cent (rare)		
1792	1 cent: without BIRCH (very rare)		

The Fugio Cent uses the device of 13 linked circles to represent the 13 states.

One of the many interesting Washington pieces issued by patriotic Americans as a tribute to an outstanding hero.

Connecticut
1785–88   1 cent: laureate bust; seated figure of Liberty...... $25.00

Massachusetts
1787–88   1 cent: Indian with bow and arrow; eagle............   30.00
1787–88   ½ cent..   40.00

New Jersey
1786–88   1 cent: horse's head and plow; shield...............   25.00
New York
1787   1 cent: laureate bust; seated figure of Liberty......   75.00

Vermont
1785–86   1 cent: hillside and plow; eye...........................   75.00
1786–88   1 cent: laureate bust; seated figure of Liberty......   50.00

38

U. S. MINT ISSUES

The following tables give a comprehensive listing of all the regular issues of the United States Mint. You will note that the values depend on various types of condition, as described on pages 12-22.

The column on the extreme left of the tables gives the quantity of coins issued in a given year. Sometimes a total figure includes several varieties lumped together. In other cases the Mint reports have broken down the quantities that apply to each variety in a given year.

Wherever it seemed essential, individual varieties issued in the same year have been listed separately and carefully described in order to distinguish them from other varieties issued in the same year.

Note also that mint marks (described on pages 31-32) play an important part in determining valuation. In most cases—but not all—the *quantity* issued by each Mint will give you the clue to the *variations in value* between the coins of the different Mints.

Half Cents

HALF CENTS — LIBERTY CAP TYPE

Quantity	Year		Fair	Very Good	Fine	Very Fine
31,934	1793		$250.00	$500.00	$850.00	$1500.00

HALF CENTS — LIBERTY CAP TYPE (continued)

Quantity	Year	Fair	Very Good	Fine	Very Fine
81,600	1794	$50.00	$125.00	$175.00	$375.00
25,600	1795 lettered edge, pole	40.00	110.00	185.00	350.00
	1795 lettered edge, 1,795	40.00	110.00	185.00	350.00
	1795 plain edge, 1,795	40.00	110.00	185.00	350.00
	1795 plain edge, no pole	40.00	110.00	185.00	350.00
115,480	1796	750.00	1750.00	2750.00	5000.00
107,048	1797 lettered edge	150.00	375.00	600.00	1200.00
	1797 plain edge	40.00	85.00	175.00	325.00
	1797 1 over 1	40.00	85.00	150.00	300.00

HALF CENTS — DRAPED BUST TYPE

Quantity	Year	Fair	Very Good	Fine	Very Fine
211,530	1800	7.50	25.00	35.00	85.00
14,366	1802 over 1800	65.00	175.00	300.00	700.00
97,900	1803	12.50	22.50	40.00	75.00
1,055,312	1804 plain 4, stems	7.50	20.00	30.00	50.00
	1804 plain 4, no stems	7.50	20.00	27.50	40.00
	1804 crosslet 4, stems	7.50	20.00	27.50	40.00
	1804 crosslet 4, no stems	7.50	20.00	27.50	40.00
	1804 spiked chin	10.00	20.00	27.50	40.00
814,464	1805 small 5, stems	35.00	100.00	225.00	500.00
	1805 large 5, stems	10.00	20.00	27.50	75.00
	1805 small 5, no stems	10.00	20.00	27.50	75.00
356,000	1806 small 6, stems	20.00	45.00	85.00	150.00
	1806 small 6, no stems	10.00	20.00	27.50	75.00
	1806 large 6, stems	10.00	20.00	27.50	75.00
476,000	1807	10.00	20.00	27.50	75.00
400,000	1808 over 7	25.00	100.00	200.00	350.00
	1808	10.00	20.00	27.50	75.00

HALF CENTS — TURBAN HEAD TYPE

Quantity	Year	Good to Very Good	Fine	Very Fine	Ext. Fine	Unc.
1,154,572 {	1809	$22.50	$32.50	$50.00	$60.00	$275.00
	1809 over 6	22.50	32.50	45.00	50.00	250.00
215,000	1810	27.50	35.00	50.00	100.00	400.00
63,140	1811	55.00	100.00	200.00	375.00	850.00
63,000	1825	17.50	27.50	35.00	50.00	225.00
234,000	1826	17.50	25.00	30.00	40.00	200.00
606,000 {	1828 12 stars	18.50	27.50	40.00	60.00	400.00
	1828 13 stars	17.50	25.00	30.00	40.00	200.00
487,000	1829	17.50	25.00	30.00	40.00	200.00
154,000	1832	17.50	25.00	30.00	40.00	225.00
120,000	1833	17.50	25.00	30.00	40.00	200.00
141,000	1834	17.50	25.00	30.00	40.00	200.00
398,000	1835	17.50	25.00	30.00	40.00	200.00

HALF CENTS — BRAIDED HAIR TYPE

39,864	1849 large date	22.50	30.00	60.00	55.00	250.00
39,812	1850	20.00	25.00	35.00	55.00	250.00
147,672	1851	18.50	25.00	30.00	45.00	225.00
129,694	1853	18.50	25.00	30.00	45.00	250.00
55,358	1854	18.50	25.00	30.00	50.00	225.00
56,500	1855	18.50	25.00	30.00	50.00	225.00
40,430	1856	18.50	25.00	35.00	52.50	225.00
35,180	1857	20.00	30.00	40.00	60.00	300.00

Large Cents

Quantity	Year	Fair to Good	Very Good	Fine	Very Fine
112,212 (all varieties)	1793 chain; AMERI	$350.00	$850.00	$1300.00	$2500.00
	1793 chain; AMERICA	300.00	750.00	1150.00	2500.00
	1793 chain; period after date	300.00	750.00	1150.00	2500.00

LARGE CENTS — WREATH TYPE

112,212	1793 wreath; vines and bars	225.00	450.00	800.00	1500.00
	1793 wreath; lettered edge	250.00	475.00	875.00	1500.00

LARGE CENTS — LIBERTY CAP TYPE

112,212	1793 Liberty Cap	400.00	800.00	1500.00	3000.00
918,521	1794	30.00	65.00	110.00	250.00
82,000	1795 lettered edge	55.00	100.00	200.00	400.00
	1795 plain edge	30.00	60.00	110.00	225.00
	*1796 Liberty Cap	37.50	90.00	150.00	300.00

* This coin is included in quantity for 1796 cents of draped bust type.

Quantity	Year	Fair to Good	Very Good	Fine	Very Fine
974,700	1796 draped bust	$35.00	$70.00	$125.00	$250.00
	1796 "LIBERTY" variety	50.00	100.00	150.00	300.00
897,510	1797	20.00	30.00	55.00	100.00
	1797 no stems on wreath	37.50	85.00	150.00	275.00
	1797 crudely milled	25.00	45.00	120.00	225.00
*	1797 with 1796 reverse	22.50	50.00	100.00	200.00
979,700	1798 over 97	20.00	55.00	125.00	250.00
	1798	12.50	25.00	45.00	85.00
*	1798 with 1796 reverse	25.00	55.00	135.00	325.00
904,585	1799 over 98	350.00	800.00	1350.00	2500.00
	1799	325.00	800.00	1300.00	2250.00
2,822,175	1800 over 1798	15.00	22.50	50.00	120.00
	1800 over 179	14.00	25.00	40.00	110.00
	1800 perfect date	12.50	22.50	40.00	85.00
	1801	11.00	20.00	40.00	90.00
**	1801 three-error variety	25.00	55.00	125.00	250.00
1,362,837	1801 fraction 1/000	15.00	30.00	75.00	140.00
	1801 1/100 over 1/000	20.00	35.00	70.00	150.00
3,435,100	1802	9.00	17.50	30.00	65.00
	1802 no stems on wreath	10.00	20.00	35.00	75.00
	1802 fraction 1/000	12.50	25.00	45.00	90.00
***	1803 small date	8.50	17.50	30.00	65.00
	1803 small date, no stems	15.00	35.00	55.00	95.00
2,471,353	1803 1/100 over 1/000	17.50	40.00	75.00	140.00
	1803 large date, fraction	60.00	125.00	215.00	375.00
	1803 large date, small fraction	100.00	250.00	400.00	650.00
756,838	1804	220.00	325.00	650.00	950.00
941,116	1805	9.00	17.50	30.00	65.00
348,000	1806	15.00	30.00	70.00	140.00
727,221	1807 over 6	10.00	22.50	35.00	75.00
	1807	9.00	17.50	35.00	65.00
	1807 comet variety	17.50	30.00	75.00	150.00

*1796 reverse has only one leaf at the tip of the right branch. The later reverses show two leaves at the tip of this branch.
**Three-error variety—fraction 1/000, no stem on the right branch and IINITED in legend.
***The small dates have blunt "1's," the large dates have pointed "1's."

43

LARGE CENTS — TURBAN HEAD TYPE

Quantity	Year		Fair to Good	Very Good	Fine	Very Fine
1,109,000 {	1808	13 stars	$12.50	$30.00	$65.00	$125.00
	1808	12 stars	13.50	32.50	65.00	150.00
222,867	1809		55.00	115.00	225.00	400.00
1,458,500 {	1810	over 9	12.50	25.00	45.00	110.00
	1810		11.00	25.00	45.00	100.00
218,025 {	1811	over 10	45.00	75.00	155.00	275.00
	1811		40.00	70.00	130.00	250.00
1,075,500	1812		10.50	20.00	45.00	110.00
418,000	1813		17.50	35.00	65.00	125.00
357,830	1814		12.50	20.00	45.00	110.00

LARGE CENTS — CORONET TYPE

Quantity	Year		Good to Very Good	Fine	Very Fine	Ext. Fine	Unc.
2,820,982	1816		7.50	12.50	25.00	45.00	210.00
3,948,400 {	1817	13 stars	7.50	12.50	25.00	45.00	210.00
	1817	15 stars	12.00	25.00	45.00	65.00	325.00
3,167,000	1818		7.00	10.00	17.50	45.00	200.00
2,671,000 {	1819	over 18	11.00	22.00	30.00	60.00	500.00
	1819		7.00	9.50	17.50	35.00	200.00
4,407,550 {	1820	over 19	10.00	20.00	27.00	55.00	210.00
	1820		7.00	9.50	17.50	40.00	200.00
389,000	1821		17.50	35.00	75.00	185.00	750.00
2,072,339	1822		7.50	12.00	22.50	45.00	300.00
855,730 {	1823	over 22	30.00	65.00	125.00	350.00	1750.00
	1823	normal date	37.50	75.00	150.00	675.00	2500.00
1,262,000 {	1824	over 22	16.50	35.00	60.00	150.00	1000.00
	1824		7.50	14.50	22.50	45.00	375.00
1,461,100	1825		7.50	14.50	22.50	45.00	275.00
1,517,425 {	1826	over 25	16.50	30.00	45.00	95.00	600.00
	1826		7.00	12.00	22.50	45.00	210.00
2,357,732	1827		7.00	9.50	17.50	40.00	210.00

Quantity	Year		Good to Very Good	Fine	Very Fine	Ext. Fine	Unc.
2,260,624 * / **	{ 1828 large date / 1828 small date		$7.00 / 12.50	$9.50 / 22.50	$17.50 / 35.00	$40.00 / 70.00	$210.00 / 350.00
1,414,500	1829		6.00	8.50	17.50	35.00	250.00
1,711,500	{ 1830 large letters / 1830 small letters		6.00 / 17.50	8.50 / 45.00	15.00 / 80.00	35.00 / 135.00	210.00 / 375.00
3,359,260	1831		6.00	8.50	15.00	30.00	210.00
2,362,000	1832		6.00	8.50	15.00	30.00	250.00
2,739,000	1833		6.00	8.50	15.00	30.00	210.00
1,755,100	1834		7.00	10.00	17.50	35.00	210.00
3,878,400	{ 1835 head of 1834 / 1835 head of 1836		6.00 / 6.00	10.00 / 10.00	15.00 / 17.50	30.00 / 35.00	210.00 / 235.00
2,111,000	1836		6.00	9.50	15.00	30.00	225.00
5,558,300	{ 1837 plain hair cord / 1837 beaded hair cord		6.00 / 6.00	8.50 / 8.50	15.00 / 15.00	30.00 / 30.00	210.00 / 210.00
6,370,200	1838		6.00	8.50	14.00	30.00	210.00

LARGE CENTS — BRAIDED HAIR TYPE

Quantity	Year		Good to Very Good	Fine	Very Fine	Ext. Fine	Unc.
3,128,661	{ 1839 over 36 / 1839 type of 38 / 1839 silly head / 1839 booby head / 1839 type of 1840		125.00 / 10.00 / 14.00 / 10.00 / 7.50	250.00 / 20.00 / 25.00 / 20.00 / 15.00	350.00 / 35.00 / 35.00 / 30.00 / 25.00	500.00 / 55.00 / 55.00 / 60.00 / 45.00	Rare / 235.00 / 400.00 / 400.00 / 210.00
2,462,700	1840		6.00	8.50	15.00	35.00	210.00
1,597,367	1841		6.00	8.50	15.00	35.00	210.00
2,383,390	1842		6.00	8.50	15.00	30.00	210.00
2,428,320	{ 1843 type of 1842 / 1843 obverse of 1842 and reverse of 1844 / 1843 type of 1844		6.00 / 25.00 / 7.00	8.50 / 60.00 / 11.50	15.00 / 80.00 / 23.50	35.00 / 150.00 / 40.00	210.00 / 650.00 / 350.00
2,397,752	1844		6.00	8.50	12.50	25.00	210.00
3,894,804	1845		6.00	8.50	11.00	20.00	185.00
4,120,800	{ 1846 tall date / 1846 small date		6.00 / 6.00	8.50 / 8.50	15.00 / 11.00	30.00 / 20.00	200.00 / 195.00
6,183,669	1847		6.00	8.50	11.00	20.00	195.00
6,415,799	1848		6.00	8.50	11.00	20.00	195.00
4,178,500	1849		6.00	8.50	11.00	20.00	210.00
4,426,844	1850		6.00	8.50	11.00	20.00	175.00
9,889,707	1851		6.00	8.50	11.00	20.00	175.00
5,063,094	1852		6.00	8.50	11.00	20.00	175.00
6,641,131	1853		6.00	8.50	11.00	20.00	175.00
4,236,156	1854		6.00	8.50	11.00	20.00	175.00
1,574,829	1855		6.00	8.50	11.00	20.00	175.00
2,690,463	1856		6.00	8.50	11.00	20.00	175.00
333,456	1857		27.50	35.00	45.00	70.00	240.00

*The "8's" of the 1828 large date have round centers.
**The "8's" of the 1828 small date have oval centers and a heavy crossbar.

Flying Eagle Cents

In 1857 the Mint discontinued the issue of half cents and large cents because there was little use for them outside large cities, and it was therefore expensive to issue them. The half cents were never resumed, but cents continued to be issued, though in reduced size.

The 1856 Flying Eagle cent is probably the best known American pattern coin. About 1,000 of these pieces dated 1856 were struck, even though the legislation authorizing the small cent was not enacted until February 21, 1857.

The 1856 issue totalled only about 1,000 pieces. Since they appeared before the 1857 authorizing law, many authorities consider them patterns rather than real issues.

Quantity	Year	Good	Very Good	Fine	Very Fine	Ext. Fine	Unc.	Proof
* 1,000	1856 rare.......	$700.00	$850.00	$1100.00	$1250.00	$1500.00	$2400.00	$2850.00

FLYING EAGLE CENTS

Quantity	Year	Good	Very Good	Fine	Very Fine	Ext. Fine	Unc.	Proof
17,450,000	1857..............	7.50	8.50	11.00	22.50	50.00	450.00	3250.00
24,600,000	1858 large letters.....	7.50	8.50	12.50	22.50	55.00	450.00	2850.00
	1858 small letters.....	7.50	8.50	12.50	22.50	55.00	450.00	2850.00

*Collectors are cautioned to examine any 1856 Flying Eagle cent very carefully. Altered date 1858's are frequently seen. On a genuine 1856 the center of the "o" in "of" is crude and nearly square. On the 1858 it is rounded. The figure "5" slants to the right on a genuine 1856 and the vertical stroke of the "5" points to the center of the ball just below. On a 1858 this vertical bar points to the left outside the ball. On an altered 1858, the lower half of the "6" is too thick. Some coins are crudely altered and the poor workmanship is obvious but others are very cleverly done and the alteration can be detected only by careful examination with a magnifying glass.

Indian Head Cents

The Flying Eagle was discontinued in 1859 in favor of the Indian Head design. The first issues from 1859 through part of 1864 were struck on thick, copper-nickel planchets. The later coins were struck on thinner bronze planchets. About 100 pattern Indian Heads dated 1858 of the later adopted design were made. These were made as specimens of the proposed new coinage and are not actual regularly issued coins. The 1859 Indian Head shows a laurel wreath on the reverse. In 1860 an oak wreath with a small shield was adopted.

1858 Indian Head cent; this was not regularly used until 1859 but about 100 pieces were dated 1858 using the later-adopted design.

Quantity	Year	Proof
100	1858	$750.00

INDIAN HEAD CENTS
(*White Copper-Nickel, thick*)

Quantity	Year	Good	Very Good	Fine	Very Fine	Ext. Fine	Unc.	Proof
36,400,000	1859	$3.50	$5.50	$9.00	$17.50	$50.00	$350.00	$600.00

20,566,000	1860	3.25	4.00	7.00	11.50	22.50	80.00	500.00
10,100,000	1861	6.50	10.00	15.00	20.00	30.00	90.00	525.00
28,075,000	1862	3.00	4.00	5.00	7.50	12.50	65.00	375.00
49,840,000	1863	2.75	3.50	4.75	7.50	12.00	65.00	350.00
13,740,000	1864	4.50	6.50	11.00	16.50	25.00	80.00	550.00

INDIAN HEAD CENTS
(*Bronze*)

Quantity	Year	Good	Very Good	Fine	Very Fine	Ext. Fine	Unc.	Proof
39,233,714	1864	$2.50	$4.00	$7.50	$15.00	$25.00	$60.00	$575.00
	1864 L on ribbon rare	11.00	22.50	40.00	62.50	82.50	225.00	5000.00
35,429,286	1865	2.25	3.25	6.50	12.50	20.00	45.00	250.00
9,826,500	1866	7.50	12.50	22.50	35.00	55.00	125.00	275.00
9,821,000	1867	7.50	12.50	22.50	35.00	55.00	125.00	275.00
10,266,500	1868	7.50	12.50	22.50	35.00	55.00	125.00	275.00
	1869 over 68	50.00	75.00	150.00	250.00	400.00	800.00	
6,420,000	1869	14.00	30.00	50.00	75.00	120.00	275.00	450.00
5,275,000	1870	13.00	22.50	40.00	55.00	80.00	165.00	275.00
3,929,500	1871	16.00	27.50	45.00	60.00	90.00	185.00	300.00
4,042,000	1872	17.50	32.50	55.00	75.00	120.00	260.00	400.00
11,676,500	1873	4.00	7.00	14.50	20.00	37.50	75.00	200.00
14,187,500	1874	4.00	7.00	14.50	20.00	37.50	75.00	200.00
13,528,000	1875	4.00	7.00	14.50	20.00	37.50	75.00	150.00
7,944,000	1876	6.50	9.00	22.50	27.50	45.00	90.00	150.00
852,500	1877	95.00	135.00	185.00	250.00	400.00	850.00	1100.00
5,799,955	1878	6.50	10.00	25.00	40.00	55.00	95.00	135.00
16,231,200	1879	1.50	2.50	6.00	12.50	17.50	45.00	100.00
38,964,955	1880	1.00	1.50	3.00	5.00	8.50	35.00	85.00
39,211,575	1881	1.00	1.50	3.00	5.00	8.50	35.00	85.00
38,581,100	1882	1.00	1.50	3.00	5.00	8.50	35.00	85.00
45,598,109	1883	1.00	1.50	3.00	5.00	8.50	35.00	85.00
23,261,742	1884	1.50	2.50	5.50	9.00	12.50	45.00	85.00
11,765,384	1885	3.00	5.25	8.50	14.00	20.00	55.00	100.00
17,654,290	1886	1.75	2.75	5.00	8.50	16.50	50.00	90.00
45,226,483	1887	.85	1.00	1.75	3.00	6.00	37.50	80.00
37,494,414	1888	.85	1.00	1.75	3.00	6.00	37.50	80.00
48,869,361	1889	.85	1.00	1.75	3.00	6.00	35.00	80.00
57,182,854	1890	.85	1.00	1.75	3.00	6.00	35.00	80.00
47,072,350	1891	.85	1.00	1.75	3.00	6.00	35.00	80.00
37,649,832	1892	.85	1.00	1.75	3.00	6.00	35.00	80.00
46,642,195	1893	.85	1.00	1.75	3.00	6.00	35.00	80.00
16,752,132	1894	1.50	3.75	6.50	10.00	15.00	40.00	90.00
38,343,636	1895	.75	.90	1.25	2.75	4.75	32.50	80.00
39,057,293	1896	.75	.90	1.25	2.75	4.75	32.50	80.00
50,466,330	1897	.75	.90	1.25	2.75	4.75	32.50	80.00
49,823,079	1898	.75	.90	1.25	2.75	4.75	32.50	80.00
53,600,031	1899	.75	.90	1.25	2.75	4.75	32.50	80.00
66,833,764	1900	.70	.85	1.15	2.00	4.00	32.50	80.00
79,611,143	1901	.70	.85	1.15	1.75	4.00	30.00	80.00
87,376,722	1902	.70	.85	1.15	1.75	4.00	30.00	80.00
85,094,493	1903	.70	.85	1.15	1.75	4.00	30.00	80.00
61,328,015	1904	.70	.85	1.15	1.75	4.00	30.00	80.00
80,719,163	1905	.70	.85	1.15	1.75	4.00	30.00	80.00
96,022,255	1906	.70	.85	1.15	1.75	4.00	30.00	80.00
108,138,618	1907	.70	.85	1.15	1.75	4.00	30.00	80.00
32,327,987	1908	.75	.90	1.25	2.00	4.00	35.00	85.00
1,115,000	1908 S	16.00	18.00	22.50	27.50	40.00	125.00	
14,370,645	1909	1.00	1.25	1.50	2.50	6.50	35.00	90.00
309,000	1909 S	60.00	70.00	80.00	95.00	145.00	295.00	

The "S" mint mark on the 1908 and 1909 issues is at the bottom of the reverse under the wreath.

48

Lincoln Head Cents

These coins have been issued in bronze since 1909. In 1943 the content was steel, and in 1944-1945 it was copper salvaged from shell cases. All years are quite inexpensive to obtain. The only notable rarity is the 1909 S issue with the initials VDB—standing for Victor D. Brenner, the designer of the coin. This variety was issued in rather a small quantity before the initials were withdrawn.

LINCOLN HEAD CENTS

The mint mark is on the obverse under the date.

Quantity	Year	Good	Very Good	Fine	Very Fine	Ext. Fine	Unc.
27,995,000	1909 VDB	$1.75	$2.00	$2.25	$2.50	$3.50	$11.00
484,000	1909 S VDB	115.00	125.00	135.00	140.00	175.00	250.00
72,702,618	1909 plain	.40	.45	.50	.60	1.50	7.50
1,825,000	1909 S plain	25.00	27.50	30.00	35.00	45.00	75.00
146,801,218	1910	.15	.25	.40	.75	1.50	9.00
6,045,000	1910 S	6.00	6.50	7.50	8.50	10.00	45.00
101,177,787	1911	.15	.30	.65	1.25	4.00	12.50
4,026,000	1911 S	10.00	11.00	12.50	15.00	20.00	60.00
12,672,000	1911 D	2.50	3.50	5.00	8.50	15.00	50.00
68,153,060	1912	.20	.40	1.65	3.75	6.00	17.50
4,431,000	1912 S	9.00	10.00	12.00	15.00	20.00	60.00
10,411,000	1912 D	2.50	3.50	5.00	10.00	20.00	60.00
76,532,352	1913	.20	.35	1.25	3.75	6.50	20.00
6,101,000	1913 S	5.00	5.50	6.50	8.00	15.00	50.00
15,804,000	1913 D	1.25	1.75	3.00	6.75	15.00	55.00
75,238,432	1914	.20	.35	1.75	4.00	7.50	32.50
4,137,000	1914 S	6.75	7.50	8.50	11.00	18.50	75.00
1,193,000	1914 D	40.00	45.00	55.00	85.00	175.00	750.00
29,092,120	1915	.60	1.00	4.50	9.00	20.00	70.00
4,833,000	1915 S	5.50	6.00	7.00	10.00	15.00	60.00
22,050,000	1915 D	.75	1.00	1.25	5.00	9.50	30.00
131,833,677	1916	.15	.20	.35	.75	2.25	10.00
22,510,000	1916 S	.50	.65	1.25	2.50	6.00	30.00
35,956,000	1916 D	.20	.35	1.00	2.75	6.50	25.00
196,429,785	1917	.15	.20	.35	.60	2.00	10.00
32,620,000	1917 S	.20	.30	.65	2.50	5.25	30.00
55,120,000	1917 D	.20	.30	.65	2.75	6.50	30.00
288,104,634	1918	.15	.20	.35	.60	2.00	12.00
34,680,000	1918 S	.20	.30	.50	2.00	4.50	35.00
47,830,000	1918 D	.20	.30	.60	2.25	5.00	32.50
392,021,000	1919	.15	.20	.30	.60	1.75	9.00
139,760,000	1919 S	.20	.30	.40	.75	2.50	17.50
57,154,000	1919 D	.20	.30	.65	2.75	5.00	20.00
310,165,000	1920	.15	.20	.30	.65	1.75	9.00
46,220,000	1920 S	.15	.20	.50	1.25	4.00	30.00
49,280,000	1920 D	.15	.20	.55	1.25	4.00	35.00
39,157,000	1921	.20	.25	.50	1.00	4.25	30.00
15,274,000	1921 S	.60	.75	1.00	2.50	9.00	175.00

Quantity	Year	Good	Very Good	Fine	Very Fine	Ext. Fine	Unc.
	1922	$45.00	$55.00	$80.00	$125.00	$225.00	$1100.00
7,160,000	1922 D	6.00	6.50	7.50	9.00	12.50	50.00
74,723,000	1923	.15	.20	.35	.60	1.75	9.00
8,700,000	1923 S	1.50	1.75	2.00	4.50	15.00	250.00
75,178,000	1924	.15	.20	.35	.60	2.50	20.00
11,696,000	1924 S	.50	.75	1.00	2.25	5.50	110.00
2,520,000	1924 D	8.00	9.00	10.00	13.50	28.00	275.00
139,949,000	1925	.15	.20	.35	.60	2.00	8.00
26,380,000	1925 S	.15	.25	.40	1.00	3.50	37.50
22,580,000	1925 D	.25	.35	.55	1.10	4.00	35.00
157,088,000	1926	.15	.20	.35	.60	2.00	7.50
4,550,000	1926 S	3.00	3.50	4.00	5.00	12.50	150.00
28,020,000	1926 D	.20	.30	.50	.80	3.00	32.50
144,440,000	1927	.15	.20	.30	.45	2.00	7.50
14,276,000	1927 S	.30	.40	.75	1.75	4.00	45.00
27,170,000	1927 D	.20	.30	.50	.75	2.00	17.50
134,116,000	1928	.15	.20	.30	.40	1.50	7.50
17,266,000	1928 S	.25	.80	.35	.90	2.25	30.00
31,170,000	1928 D	.20	.25	.30	.60	1.50	17.50
185,262,000	1929	.15	.20	.30	.50	1.25	6.50
50,148,000	1929 S	.15	.20	.30	.50	1.25	7.00
41,730,000	1929 D	.15	.20	.30	.50	1.25	8.00
157,415,000	1930	.10	.15	.20	.35	1.00	4.50
24,286,000	1930 S	.10	.15	.20	.50	1.50	7.00
40,100,000	1930 D	.10	.15	.20	.45	1.00	7.50
19,396,000	1931	.20	.25	.30	.55	1.50	15.00
866,000	1931 S	23.00	24.00	25.00	27.00	30.00	50.00
4,480,000	1931 D	2.75	3.25	3.50	4.00	7.00	55.00
9,062,000	1932	1.00	1.25	1.50	2.00	2.75	15.00
10,500,000	1932 D	.65	.75	1.25	2.00	2.00	14.00
14,360,000	1933	.50	.60	.70	.90	2.00	17.50
6,200,000	1933 D	1.75	2.00	2.25	2.50	3.00	20.00

Quantity	Year	Unc.	Quantity	Year	Unc.
219,080,000	1934	$3.00	282,760,000	1944 S copper	$ .35
28,446,000	1934 D	17.50	430,587,000	1944 D copper	.30
245,388,000	1935	1.75	1,040,515,000	1945 copper	.30
38,702,000	1935 S	4.50	181,770,000	1945 S copper	.50
47,000,000	1935 D	2.50	226,268,000	1945 D copper	.60
309,637,569	1936	1.50	991,655,000	1946	.20
29,130,000	1936 S	2.00	198,100,000	1946 S	.50
40,620,000	1936 D	1.75	315,690,000	1946 D	.25
309,179,320	1937	1.50	190,555,000	1947	.60
34,500,000	1937 S	2.00	99,000,000	1947 S	.70
50,430,000	1937 D	1.75	194,750,000	1947 D	.35
156,696,734	1938	1.85	317,570,000	1948	.50
15,180,000	1938 S	4.00	81,735,000	1948 S	1.00
20,010,000	1938 D	3.00	172,637,500	1948 D	.30
316,479,520	1939	1.25	217,490,000	1949	.75
52,070,000	1939 S	1.75	64,290,000	1949 S	1.40
15,160,000	1939 D	5.00	154,370,500	1949 D	.60
586,825,872	1940	1.00	272,686,386	1950	.40
112,940,000	1940 S	.85	118,505,000	1950 S	.65
81,390,000	1940 D	1.00	334,950,000	1950 D	.30
887,039,100	1941	.75	294,633,500	1951	1.50
92,360,000	1941 S	4.00	100,890,000	1951 S	.90
128,700,000	1941 D	3.00	625,355,000	1951 D	.20
657,828,600	1942	.50	186,856,980	1952	.50
85,590,000	1942 S	5.00	137,800,004	1952 S	.65
206,698,000	1942 D	.70	746,130,000	1952 D	.20
684,628,670	1943 zinc-steel	.60	256,883,800	1953	.20
191,550,000	1943 S zinc-steel	1.75	181,835,000	1953 S	.45
217,660,000	1943 D zinc-steel	.75	700,515,000	1953 D	.20
1,435,400,000	1944 copper	.25	71,873,350	1954	.50

Quantity	Year	Unc.
96,190,000	1954 S	$ .40
251,552,500	1954 D	.25
330,958,200	1955	.20

1955 Double die
VF 220.00   Unc. 450.00

Quantity	Year	Unc.
44,610,000	1955 S	.50
563,257,500	1955 D	.20
420,926,081	1956	.15
1,098,201,100	1956 D	.15
282,540,000	1957	.15
1,051,342,000	1957 D	.15
252,595,000	1958	.15
800,953,300	1958 D	.10
619,715,000	1959	.10
1,279,760,000	1959 D	.10
586,405,000 {	1960 Small date	4.25
	1960 Large date	.10
1,580,884,000 {	1960 D Small date	.30
	1960 D Large date	.10
756,373,244	1961	.10
1,753,266,700	1961 D	.10
609,263,019	1962	.10
1,793,148,400	1962 D	.10
757,185,645	1963	.10
1,774,020,400	1963 D	.10

Quantity	Year	Unc.
2,648,575,000	1964	$ .10
3,799,071,500	1964 D	.10
1,494,884,900	1965	.10
2,185,886,200	1966	.10
3,048,667,100	1967	.10
1,707,880,970	1968	.10
2,886,269,600	1968 D	.10
258,270,001	1968 S	.10
1,136,910,000	1969	.10
4,002,832,200	1969 D	.10
544,375,000	1969 S	.10
1,898,315,000	1970	.10
2,891,438,900	1970 D	.10
693,192,814	1970 S	.10
1,919,490,000	1971	.10
2,911,045,600	1971 D	.10
528,354,192	1971 S	.10
	1972 Double strike	115.00
2,933,255,000	1972	.10
2,665,071,400	1972 D	.10
380,200,104	1972 S	.10
3,728,245,000	1973	.10
3,549,576,588	1973 D	.10
319,937,634	1973 S	.10
4,232,140,523	1974	.10
4,235,098,000	1974 D	.10
	1974 S	
	1975	
	1975 D	
	1975 S	

Two Cent Pieces

Quantity	Year	Good to Very Good	Fine	Very Fine	Ext. Fine	Unc.	Proof
19,847,500 {	1864 small motto	$45.00	$70.00	$90.00	$120.00	$375.00	
	1864 large motto	5.50	7.50	12.00	25.00	150.00	$420.00
13,640,000	1865	5.50	7.50	12.00	25.00	150.00	360.00
3,177,000	1866	5.50	7.50	12.00	25.00	160.00	350.00
2,938,750	1867	5.50	7.50	12.00	25.00	160.00	350.00
2,803,750	1868	5.50	7.50	12.00	25.00	160.00	350.00
1,546,500	1869	5.50	7.50	12.00	25.00	160.00	360.00
861,250	1870	6.50	10.00	15.00	30.00	175.00	370.00
721,250	1871	7.00	11.00	17.50	35.00	185.00	375.00
65,000	1872	35.00	50.00	60.00	80.00	200.00	475.00
?	1873 only proofs were struck						825.00

Three Cent Pieces

1851-1853   1854-1873

The "O" mint mark is to the right of the "III" on the reverse.

Quantity	Year	Good to Very Good	Fine	Very Fine	Ext. Fine	Unc.	Proof
5,447,400	1851	$8.50	$13.00	$20.00	$32.50	$150.00	
720,000	1851 O	12.50	20.00	35.00	55.00	250.00	
18,663,500	1852	8.50	13.00	20.00	30.00	135.00	
11,400,000	1853	8.50	13.00	20.00	30.00	135.00	
671,000	1854	13.00	20.00	30.00	60.00	500.00	
139,000	1855	15.00	27.00	50.00	125.00	650.00	$2500.00
1,458,000	1856	13.00	20.00	30.00	60.00	485.00	2500.00
1,042,000	1857	11.00	16.00	25.00	60.00	475.00	2000.00
1,604,000	1858	11.00	16.00	25.00	60.00	500.00	1250.00
365,000	1859	12.00	16.00	25.00	35.00	150.00	325.00
287,000	1860	12.00	16.00	25.00	35.00	150.00	325.00
498,000	1861	12.00	16.00	25.00	35.00	145.00	325.00
363,550	1862	12.00	16.00	25.00	35.00	145.00	350.00
21,460	1863 (all remaining years struck as proofs only)						425.00
470	1864						425.00
8,500	1865						425.00
22,725	1866						350.00
4,625	1867						375.00
4,100	1868						350.00
5,100	1869						350.00
4,000	1870						350.00
4,260	1871						350.00
1,950	1872						350.00
600	1873						425.00

Quantity	Year	Good to Very Good	Fine	Very Fine	Ext. Fine	Unc.	Proof
11,382,000	1865	$5.00	$7.00	$9.00	$14.00	$80.00	$600.00
4,801,000	1866	5.00	7.00	9.00	14.00	80.00	200.00
3,915,000	1867	5.00	7.00	9.00	14.00	85.00	140.00
3,252,000	1868	5.00	7.00	9.00	14.00	85.00	140.00
1,604,000	1869	5.00	7.50	9.50	14.00	85.00	140.00
1,335,000	1870	5.00	7.00	9.00	15.00	85.00	140.00
604,000	1871	5.50	8.00	10.00	15.00	90.00	140.00
862,000	1872	5.00	7.00	10.00	15.00	90.00	125.00
1,173,000	1873	5.50	7.50	10.00	14.00	90.00	130.00
790,000	1874	5.50	7.50	10.00	14.00	90.00	135.00
228,000	1875	6.50	10.00	13.50	20.00	95.00	135.00
162,000	1876	7.50	9.00	13.00	20.00	100.00	140.00
?	1877 only proofs were struck						700.00
2,350	1878 only proofs were struck						275.00
41,200	1879	17.50	25.00	30.00	35.00	110.00	140.00
24,955	1880	18.50	27.50	35.00	40.00	110.00	140.00
1,080,575	1881	5.00	7.00	9.00	14.00	85.00	135.00
25,300	1882	18.50	27.50	35.00	40.00	120.00	140.00
10,609	1883	22.50	40.00	45.00	50.00	150.00	140.00
5,642	1884	30.00	45.00	50.00	60.00	200.00	175.00
4,790	1885	35.00	50.00	60.00	70.00	220.00	180.00
4,290	1886 only proofs were struck						200.00
7,961	1887	40.00	55.00	65.00	75.00	200.00	225.00
	1887 over 86—only proofs were struck						150.00
41,083	1888	17.50	25.00	30.00	35.00	100.00	140.00
21,561	1889	18.50	30.00	35.00	40.00	100.00	140.00

These now obsolete denominations were each introduced to fill a specific need. The two cent piece was an attempt to cope with the desperate shortage of small coins that occurred near the close of the Civil War. The theory was that a coin press could produce just as many two cent pieces as one cent pieces in a given time, but the face value of the coins going into circulation would be double. Once the deficiency was made up, the larger coins proved to be awkward. The silver three cent piece came into being along with the 3¢ letter rate with the thought that it would be convenient for buying stamps. The nickel three cent piece which came later was intended to redeem the three cent paper notes issued during the Civil War. Neither of the three cent coins was really practical and after the first few years they were struck in small quantities only until they were finally discontinued.

Nickel Five Cents

Though nickel was suggested for American coins as early as 1837, the first five-cent nickels were not issued until 1866.

NICKEL FIVE CENTS — SHIELD TYPE

1866 - 1867   1867 - 1883

Quantity	Year	Good to Very Good	Fine	Very Fine	Ext. Fine	Unc.	Proof
14,742,500	1866	$11.00	$17.00	$25.00	$60.00	$300.00	$1250.00
30,909,500 {	1867 with rays	13.50	25.00	35.00	60.00	325.00	
	1867 without rays	8.00	11.00	15.00	24.00	85.00	130.00
28,817,000	1868	8.00	11.00	15.00	24.00	85.00	130.00
16,395,000	1869	8.00	11.00	15.00	24.00	90.00	130.00
4,806,000	1870	9.00	12.00	17.00	27.50	90.00	130.00
561,000	1871	30.00	40.00	50.00	80.00	225.00	300.00
6,036,000	1872	8.50	11.00	15.00	22.00	90.00	130.00
4,550,000	1873	9.00	12.00	17.00	25.00	85.00	130.00
3,538,000	1874	10.00	15.00	18.00	27.50	90.00	135.00
2,097,000	1875	12.00	20.00	25.00	40.00	135.00	175.00
2,530,000	1876	11.00	17.50	22.50	30.00	95.00	140.00
?500	1877 only proofs were struck						950.00
2,350	1878 only proofs were struck						275.00
29,100	1879	24.00	30.00	40.00	55.00	175.00	150.00
19,955	1880	27.50	35.00	45.00	60.00	180.00	160.00
72,375	1881	27.50	40.00	45.00	60.00	175.00	160.00
11,476,600	1882	8.50	11.00	15.00	22.00	85.00	130.00
1,456,919	1883	8.50	11.00	15.00	22.00	85.00	130.00

LIBERTY HEAD NICKELS

1883   1883-1912

The variety without "CENTS" was issued first, but unscrupulous people goldplated them and passed them off as $5 gold pieces. To remedy the situation, the word "CENTS" was added to the later issues and continued to appear on subsequent dates.

LIBERTY HEAD NICKELS

Quantity	Year	Good	Very Good	Fine	Very Fine	Ext. Fine	Unc.	Proof
5,479,519	1883 without "Cents"....	$1.50	$2.00	$2.50	$3.00	$8.50	$45.00	$160.00
16,032,983	1883 with "Cents"....	3.50	5.00	8.00	12.50	18.50	70.00	125.00
11,273,942	1884..................	4.50	7.00	9.00	15.00	75.00	75.00	125.00
1,476,490	1885..................	65.00	90.00	110.00	130.00	165.00	320.00	325.00
3,330,290	1886..................	30.00	40.00	55.00	60.00	85.00	175.00	200.00
15,263,652	1887..................	2.75	4.00	7.50	10.00	15.00	70.00	115.00
10,720,483	1888..................	5.00	7.00	10.00	14.00	18.50	75.00	120.00
15,881,361	1889..................	2.50	4.00	7.00	9.00	15.00	70.00	115.00
16,259,272	1890..................	3.75	5.00	10.00	10.00	15.00	70.00	115.00
16,834,350	1891..................	2.75	4.00	7.00	8.00	14.50	70.00	115.00
11,699,642	1892..................	2.75	4.00	7.00	8.00	14.50	70.00	115.00
13,370,195	1893..................	2.75	4.00	7.00	8.00	14.50	70.00	115.00
5,413,132	1894..................	4.50	6.50	9.00	10.00	18.50	80.00	125.00
9,979,884	1895..................	1.75	3.00	6.50	8.00	14.50	70.00	115.00
8,842,920	1896..................	2.00	4.00	7.50	10.00	17.50	80.00	130.00
20,428,735	1897..................	.90	1.50	2.75	4.50	9.00	70.00	115.00
12,532,087	1898..................	.90	1.50	2.50	5.00	9.00	70.00	115.00
26,029,031	1899..................	.75	1.50	2.50	4.50	9.00	70.00	115.00
27,255,995	1900..................	.65	.80	1.50	4.00	8.75	65.00	110.00
26,480,213	1901..................	.65	.80	1.50	4.00	8.75	65.00	110.00
31,480,579	1902..................	.65	.80	1.50	4.00	8.75	65.00	110.00
28,006,725	1903..................	.65	.80	1.50	4.00	8.75	65.00	110.00
21,404,984	1904..................	.65	.80	1.50	4.00	8.75	65.00	110.00
29,827,276	1905..................	.65	.80	1.50	4.00	8.75	65.00	110.00
38,613,725	1906..................	.65	.80	1.50	4.00	8.75	65.00	110.00
39,214,800	1907..................	.65	.80	1.50	4.00	8.75	65.00	125.00
22,686,177	1908..................	.65	.80	1.50	4.00	8.75	65.00	110.00
11,590,526	1909..................	.65	.80	2.00	4.50	8.75	65.00	110.00
30,169,353	1910..................	.65	.80	1.50	4.00	8.75	65.00	110.00
39,559,372	1911..................	.65	.80	1.50	4.00	8.75	65.00	110.00
26,236,714	1912..................	.65	.80	1.50	4.00	8.75	65.00	110.00
8,474,000	*1912 D	1.40	2.25	7.00	12.50	47.50	225.00	
238,000	*1912 S..............	27.50	32.50	45.00	60.00	110.00	425.00	
?	1913 (an outstanding rarity)							

* Mint mark to left of "CENTS" on reverse.

BUFFALO NICKELS

The mint marks are under "Five cents" on the reverse.

1913   1913-1938

Quantity	Year	Good	Very Good	Fine	Very Fine	Ext. Fine	Unc.
30,993,520	1913 Type 1—buffalo on mound	$2.00	$2.50	$3.00	$4.25	$9.50	$28.50
2,105,000	1913 S Type 1 ..	5.00	6.50	9.00	11.00	16.00	40.00
5,337,000	1913 D Type 1..	4.25	4.75	5.50	6.50	11.00	35.00
29,858,700	1913 Type 2—buffalo on line ...	2.50	3.00	3.50	4.00	6.00	25.00
1,209,000	1913 S Type 2 ..	27.50	35.00	45.00	50.00	70.00	125.00
4,156,000	1913 D Type 2..	20.00	25.00	32.50	35.00	45.00	70.00

Quantity	Year	Good	Very Good	Fine	Very Fine	Ext. Fine	Unc.
20,665,738	1914	$3.00	$4.00	$5.00	$6.00	$9.00	$30.00
3,470,000	1914 S	4.00	5.00	8.00	11.00	18.50	70.00
3,912,000	1914 D	16.00	20.00	28.00	32.50	50.00	115.00
20,987,270	1915	1.25	1.75	3.00	4.00	10.00	27.50
1,505,000	1915 S	6.00	10.00	20.00	30.00	47.50	130.00
7,569,500	1915 D	4.75	6.00	10.00	15.00	25.00	65.00
63,498,066	1916	.50	.85	1.50	2.00	6.00	20.00
11,860,000	1916 S	2.25	3.50	5.50	8.50	20.00	65.00
13,333,000	1916 D	3.50	4.50	6.50	9.00	19.00	65.00
51,424,029	1917	.60	.80	1.00	2.00	10.00	30.00
4,193,000	1917 S	2.50	5.50	9.00	17.50	40.00	120.00
9,910,800	1917 D	2.75	5.50	9.00	23.00	40.00	100.00
32,086,314	1918	.50	1.00	2.00	3.75	12.00	50.00
4,882,000	1918 S	2.50	5.00	9.50	25.00	50.00	155.00
8,362,000	1918 D	3.25	6.00	10.00	20.00	50.00	165.00
	1918 D over 7	140.00	225.00	450.00	750.00	1350.00	6500.00
60,868,000	1919	.50	.65	1.25	2.25	7.00	30.00
7,521,000	1919 S	2.00	5.00	10.00	22.50	67.50	210.00
8,006,000	1919 D	3.00	6.00	15.00	35.00	72.50	220.00
63,093,000	1920	.40	.60	1.15	2.00	7.00	30.00
9,689,000	1920 S	1.50	2.50	6.00	20.00	45.00	195.00
9,418,000	1920 D	2.50	4.75	9.00	27.50	50.00	200.00
10,663,000	1921	.75	1.00	3.00	6.00	12.00	65.00
1,557,000	1921 S	7.50	15.00	30.00	60.00	95.00	335.00
35,715,000	1923	.40	.60	1.15	2.00	7.00	30.00
6,142,000	1923 S	1.50	2.50	6.00	20.00	45.00	150.00
21,620,000	1924	.40	.60	1.15	3.00	7.50	50.00
1,437,000	1924 S	4.00	6.00	14.00	45.00	125.00	700.00
5,258,000	1924 D	2.00	3.00	8.00	25.00	50.00	220.00
35,565,100	1925	.40	.60	1.15	2.00	6.00	30.00
6,256,000	1925 S	2.00	4.00	6.00	15.00	45.00	250.00
4,450,000	1925 D	3.25	5.25	12.00	35.00	55.00	250.00
44,693,000	1926	.40	.55	1.00	1.25	5.00	20.00
970,000	1926 S	5.00	7.75	13.00	38.00	140.00	525.00
5,638,000	1926 D	1.75	3.75	8.50	22.50	60.00	200.00
37,981,000	1927	.40	.55	1.00	1.25	4.50	19.00
3,430,000	1927 S	.85	1.50	4.00	9.50	45.00	230.00
5,730,000	1927 D	.75	1.50	2.75	9.50	18.00	50.00
23,411,000	1928	.35	.45	.75	1.00	4.00	20.00
6,936,000	1928 S	.60	.85	1.75	2.00	9.00	55.00
6,436,000	1928 D	.55	.70	1.00	2.00	6.00	20.00
36,446,000	1929	.35	.50	.75	1.00	2.75	15.00
7,754,000	1929 S	.45	.55	.95	1.25	3.50	17.50
8,370,000	1929 D	.45	.65	1.00	1.50	3.75	20.00
22,849,000	1930	.35	.45	.75	1.00	2.25	15.00
5,435,000	1930 S	.60	.75	1.50	1.75	5.50	40.00
1,200,000	1931 S	3.50	4.00	5.00	6.00	9.50	65.00
20,213,000	1934	.30	.40	.65	1.00	3.50	20.00
7,480,003	1934 D	.45	.50	.75	1.25	4.00	27.50
58,264,000	1935	.30	.40	.50	.65	1.25	12.50
10,300,000	1935 S	.35	.40	.50	1.00	1.95	16.00
12,092,000	1935 D	.40	.45	.65	1.25	2.25	22.50
119,001,420	1936				.55	1.10	11.50
14,930,000	1936 S				.55	1.60	12.50
24,418,000	1936 D				.55	1.60	12.50
79,485,769	1937				.55	1.00	11.50
5,635,000	1937 S				.65	1.25	11.50
17,826,000	1937 D				.60	1.50	11.50
	1937 D three-legged buffalo				50.00	70.00	310.00
7,020,000	1938 D				1.25	1.75	9.00

JEFFERSON NICKELS

The mint marks are to the right of the building or above it on the reverse until 1968, then on the obverse near the date.

Quantity	Year	Ext. Fine	Unc.
19,515,365	1938	$ .55	$1.50
4,105,000	1938 S	3.25	7.75
5,376,000	1938 D	2.25	6.00
120,627,535	1939	.35	1.25
6,630,000	1939 S	2.50	13.00
3,514,000	1939 D	9.00	50.00
176,499,158	1940	.35	.75
39,690,000	1940 S	.50	1.75
43,540,000	1940 D	.40	1.50
203,283,720	1941	.30	1.00
43,445,000	1941 S	.40	1.50
53,432,000	1941 D	.40	1.50
49,818,600	1942	.40	1.50
13,938,000	1942 D	2.00	13.50

Wartime Silver Content

Quantity	Year	Ext. Fine	Unc.
57,900,600	1942 P	4.00	13.50
32,900,000	1942 S	2.00	5.50
271,165,000	1943 P	1.25	2.75
104,060,000	1943 S	1.25	3.00
15,294,000	1943 D	2.50	4.00
119,150,000	1944 P	1.25	2.50
21,640,000	1944 S	1.50	2.75
32,309,000	1944 D	1.50	3.50
119,408,100	1945 P	1.25	2.50
58,939,000	1945 S	1.15	2.15
37,158,000	1945 D	1.15	2.15

Prewar Nickel Content

Quantity	Year	Unc.
161,116,000	1946	.45
13,560,000	1946 S	1.35
45,292,200	1946 D	.75
95,000,000	1947	.40
24,720,000	1947 S	1.25
37,822,000	1947 D	1.00
89,348,000	1948	.50
11,300,000	1948 S	1.50
44,734,000	1948 D	1.30
60,652,000	1949	.60
9,716,000	1949 S	2.75
35,238,000	1949 D	1.00
9,847,386	1950	2.50
2,630,030	1950 D	14.00
26,689,500	1951	1.10
7,776,000	1951 S	3.75
20,460,000	1951 D	2.00
64,069,980	1952	.55
20,572,000	1952 S	.85
30,638,000	1952 D	2.25
46,772,800	1953	.30
19,210,900	1953 S	.65
59,878,600	1953 D	.60

Quantity	Year	Unc.
47,917,350	1954	$.25
29,384,000	1954 S	.30
117,183,060	1954 D	.25
8,266,200	1955	1.50
74,464,100	1955 D	.30
35,397,081	1956	.25
67,222,040	1956 D	.25
38,408,000	1957	.25
136,828,900	1957 D	.20
17,088,000	1958	.50
168,249,120	1958 D	.20
27,248,000	1959	.35
160,738,240	1959 D	.15
55,416,000	1960	.15
192,582,180	1960 D	.15
76,668,244	1961	.15
229,372,760	1961 D	.15
100,602,019	1962	.15
280,195,720	1962 D	.15
178,851,645	1963	.15
276,829,460	1963 D	.15
1,024,672,000	1964	.15
1,787,297,160	1964 D	.15
133,771,380	1965	.15
153,946,700	1966	.15
107,325,800	1967	.15
91,227,880	1968 D	.15
100,396,001	1968 S	.15
202,807,500	1969 D	.15
120,164,000	1969 S	.15
515,485,380	1970 D	.15
241,464,814	1970 S	.15
106,884,000	1971	.15
316,144,800	1971 D	.15
3,224,138	1971 S (proof only)	
202,036,000	1972	.15
351,694,600	1972 D	.15
3,267,667	1972 S (proof only)	
384,396,000	1973	.15
261,405,400	1973 D	.15
2,769,624	1973 S (proof only)	
601,752,000	1974	.15
277,373,000	1974 D	.15
2,617,350	1974 S (proof only)	
	1975	
	1975 D	
	1975 S (proof only)	

Half Dimes

HALF DIMES — FLOWING HAIR TYPE

Quantity	Year	Fair to Good	Very Good	Fine	Very Fine
86,416 {	1794	$165.00	$300.00	$475.00	$700.00
	1795	150.00	235.00	350.00	600.00

HALF DIMES — DRAPED BUST TYPE

	1796-1797	1800-1805

Quantity	Year				
10,230 {	1796	230.00	350.00	415.00	725.00
	1796 over 5	315.00	525.00	650.00	1150.00
44,527 {	1797 13 stars	230.00	350.00	415.00	625.00
	1797 15 stars	220.00	325.00	385.00	600.00
	1797 16 stars	220.00	325.00	385.00	600.00
24,000 {	1800	135.00	225.00	325.00	480.00
	1800 LIBEKTY	135.00	225.00	325.00	480.00
33,910	1801	135.00	225.00	325.00	500.00
13,010	1802 extremely rare	1500.00	3000.00	5000.00	7000.00
37,850	1803	135.00	225.00	300.00	480.00
15,600	1805	155.00	275.00	465.00	875.00

HALF DIMES — CAPPED BUST TYPE

Quantity	Year	Good to Very Good	Fine	Very Fine	Ext. Fine	Unc.
1,230,000	1829	18.50	25.00	32.50	60.00	325.00
1,240,000	1830	18.50	25.00	32.50	60.00	310.00
1,242,700	1831	18.50	25.00	32.50	60.00	310.00
965,000	1832	18.50	25.00	32.50	60.00	310.00
1,370,000	1833	18.50	25.00	32.50	60.00	310.00
1,480,000	1834	18.50	25.00	32.50	60.00	310.00
2,760,000	1835	18.50	25.00	32.50	60.00	310.00
1,900,000	1836	18.50	25.00	32.50	60.00	310.00
2,276,000 {	1837 large 5c	18.50	25.00	32.50	60.00	310.00
	1837 small 5c	22.50	45.00	65.00	100.00	850.00

HALF DIMES — LIBERTY SEATED TYPE

1837-1838   1838-1859

The mint marks are under the wreath, or within it, on the reverse.

Quantity	Year	Good to Very Good	Fine	Very Fine	Ext. Fine	Unc.
		Without stars				
2,255,000	1837	$40.00	$60.00	$80.00	$145.00	$575.00
?	1838 O	50.00	85.00	130.00	210.00	700.00
		With stars, no drapery from elbow				
2.255,000	1838	7.00	9.00	14.50	35.00	250.00
1,069,150	1839	7.00	9.00	14.50	35.00	250.00
1,096,550	1839 O	7.50	10.00	17.50	40.00	275.00
1,344,085**1840	1840	7.00	9.00	14.50	35.00	250.00
935,000**1840 O	1840 O	8.00	15.00	25.00	50.00	350.00

** Includes 1840 half dimes with drapery from elbow

		With drapery from elbow				
	1840	6.50	8.50	14.00	25.00	190.00
	1840 O	9.00	15.00	30.00	60.00	250.00
1,150,000	1841	6.50	8.50	12.50	25.00	190.00
815,000	1841 O	7.00	11.00	20.00	45.00	300.00
815,000	1842	6.50	8.50	12.50	25.00	190.00
350,000	1842 O	10.50	20.00	35.00	60.00	375.00
1,165,000	1843	6.50	8.50	12.50	25.00	190.00
430,000	1844	6.50	10.00	15.00	30.00	225.00
220,000	1844 O	10.00	20.00	40.00	75.00	325.00
1,564,000	1845	6.50	8.50	12.50	25.00	190.00
27,000	1846	55.00	80.00	125.00	275.00	750.00
1,274,000	1847	6.50	8.50	12.50	25.00	190.00
668,000	1848	6.50	8.50	12.50	25.00	190.00
600,000	1848 O	9.50	17.50	30.00	62.50	225.00
1,309,000 { 1849	1849	6.50	8.50	12.50	25.00	190.00
	1849 over 48	6.50	10.00	15.00	30.00	195.00
140,000	1849 O	35.00	67.50	100.00	175.00	650.00
955,000	1850	6.50	8.50	12.50	25.00	195.00
690,000	1850 O	7.00	12.50	25.00	40.00	275.00
781,000	1851	6.50	8.50	12.50	25.00	195.00
860,000	1851 O	7.00	12.50	25.00	40.00	325.00
1,000,500	1852	6.50	8.50	12.50	25.00	195.00
260,000	1852 O	8.50	17.50	35.00	55.00	275.00
13,345,020 { 1853 no arrows	1853 no arrows	12.50	25.00	40.00	75.00	400.00
	1853 arrows	6.50	9.00	15.00	30.00	250.00
2,360,000 { 1853 O no arrows	1853 O no arrows	90.00	140.00	200.00	320.00	750.00
	1853 O arrows	7.00	9.50	20.00	35.00	275.00
5,740,000	1854 arrows	7.00	9.00	15.00	30.00	250.00
1,560,000	1854 O arrows	7.00	9.50	17.50	35.00	275.00
1,750,000	1855 arrows	7.00	9.00	15.00	35.00	255.00
600,000	1855 O arrows	8.00	12.50	25.00	50.00	300.00
4,880,000	1856	6.50	8.50	12.50	25.00	190.00
1,100,000	1856 O	6.50	8.50	14.00	25.00	220.00
7,280,000	1857	6.50	8.00	12.50	25.00	190.00
1,380,000	1857 O	6.50	8.50	14.00	30.00	220.00
3,500,000	1858	6.50	8.50	12.50	25.00	190.00
1,660,000	1858 O	6.50	8.50	12.50	25.00	220.00
340,000	1859	7.50	12.00	17.50	30.00	225.00
560,000	1859 O	6.50	9.50	15.00	30.00	220.00

1860-1873

Quantity	Year	Good to Very Good	Fine	Very Fine	Ext. Fine	Unc.
799,000	1860 no stars	$6.50	$8.00	$12.00	$20.00	$145.00
1,060,000	1860 O	6.50	8.50	14.00	25.00	150.00
3,281,000	1861	6.50	8.00	12.00	20.00	135.00
1,492,550	1862	6.50	8.00	12.00	20.00	135.00
18,460	1863	27.50	35.00	45.00	65.00	350.00
100,000	1863 S	17.50	25.00	40.00	75.00	300.00
48,470	1864	(Rare, proof condition $450)				
90,000	1864 S	16.50	25.00	37.50	70.00	300.00
13,500	1865	25.00	35.00	45.00	75.00	400.00
120,000	1865 S	11.00	17.50	30.00	40.00	300.00
10,725	1866	25.00	32.50	42.50	75.00	400.00
120,000	1866 S	10.00	20.00	30.00	70.00	300.00
8,625	1867	27.50	35.00	45.00	75.00	400.00
120,000	1867 S	10.00	20.00	30.00	50.00	300.00
85,900	1868	9.00	15.00	22.50	30.00	135.00
280,000	1868 S	7.50	12.00	20.00	35.00	150.00
208,600	1869	7.50	12.00	17.50	27.50	135.00
230,000	1869 S	7.50	11.00	17.50	30.00	150.00
536,600	1870	6.00	8.00	12.00	20.00	135.00
1,488,860	1871	6.00	8.00	12.00	20.00	135.00
161,000	1871 S	12.50	20.00	35.00	50.00	200.00
2,947,950	1872	6.00	8.00	12.00	20.00	135.00
837,000 {	1872 S in wreath	6.00	8.00	12.00	20.00	135.00
	1872 S below wreath	6.00	8.00	14.00	25.00	150.00
712,600	1873	6.00	8.00	12.00	20.00	135.00
324,000	1873 S	6.00	8.00	14.00	25.00	150.00

Dimes

DIMES — DRAPED BUST TYPE

1795-1797   1798-1807

Quantity	Year	Fair to Good	Very Good	Fine	Very Fine
22,135	1796	$275.00	$475.00	$750.00	$1275.00
25,261 {	1797 13 stars	235.00	375.00	625.00	1025.00
	1797 16 stars	250.00	400.00	650.00	1025.00
27,550 {	1798 over 97	105.00	185.00	300.00	500.00
	1798	105.00	185.00	300.00	500.00
21,760	1800	95.00	145.00	230.00	400.00
34,640	1801	95.00	175.00	280.00	500.00
10,975	1802	110.00	210.00	340.00	625.00
33,040	1803	100.00	185.00	280.00	475.00
8,265	1804	125.00	210.00	365.00	750.00
120,780	1805	85.00	140.00	190.00	330.00
165,000	1807	85.00	130.00	190.00	320.00

DIMES — CAPPED BUST TYPE

Quantity	Year	Fair to Good	Very Good	Fine	Very Fine	Unc.
44,710	1809	$45.00	$90.00	$120.00	$210.00	$1850.00
65,180	1811 over 09	30.00	50.00	70.00	125.00	1750.00
421,500	1814	16.50	27.50	35.00	60.00	1500.00
942,587	1820	15.00	20.00	27.50	55.00	1500.00
1,186,512	1821	15.00	20.00	27.50	50.00	1500.00
100,000	1822	40.00	90.00	175.00	275.00	2500.00
440,000	1823 over 22	16.50	24.00	32.50	60.00	1600.00
?	1824 over 22	12.50	27.50	37.50	70.00	1600.00
510,000	1825	15.00	20.00	27.50	50.00	1500.00
1,215,000	1827	15.00	20.00	27.50	45.00	1500.00
125,000 {	1828 large date	22.50	35.00	60.00	100.00	1250.00
	1828 small date	17.50	25.00	35.00	55.00	1250.00

Quantity	Year	Good to Very Good	Fine	Very Fine	Ext. Fine	Unc.
770,000 {	1829 large 10c	20.00	30.00	40.00	85.00	950.00
	1829 medium 10c	16.50	24.00	35.00	70.00	950.00
	1829 small 10c	16.50	24.00	35.00	70.00	950.00
510,000	1830	16.50	24.00	32.50	55.00	850.00
771,350	1831	16.50	24.00	32.50	55.00	850.00
522,500	1832	16.50	24.00	32.50	55.00	850.00
485,000	1833	16.50	24.00	32.50	55.00	850.00
635,000	1834	16.50	24.00	32.50	55.00	850.00
1,410,000	1835	16.50	24.00	32.50	55.00	850.00
1,190,000	1836	16.50	24.00	32.50	55.00	850.00
1,042,000*	1837	16.50	24.00	32.50	55.00	850.00

* Includes Liberty Seated dimes of 1837

DIMES — LIBERTY SEATED TYPE

1837-1838   1838-1860

The mint marks are under the wreath or within it, on the reverse.

Without stars

Quantity	Year					
	1837	40.00	75.00	125.00	225.00	1600.00
402,434	1838 O	47.50	110.00	180.00	325.00	2000.00

Quantity	Year	Good to Very Good	Fine	Very Fine	Ext. Fine	Unc.

With stars, no drapery from elbow

Quantity	Year	Good to Very Good	Fine	Very Fine	Ext. Fine	Unc.
1,992,500	1838	$11.00	$19.50	$30.00	$50.00	$350.00
1,053,115	1839	5.50	8.00	14.50	35.00	325.00
1,243,272	1839 O	6.50	12.50	20.00	40.00	375.00
1,358,580**	1840	5.50	8.00	14.00	35.00	325.00
1,175,000	1840 O	7.50	12.50	20.00	40.00	375.00
	1841 very rare					

** Includes 1840 dimes with drapery from elbow

With drapery from elbow

Quantity	Year	Good to Very Good	Fine	Very Fine	Ext. Fine	Unc.
	1840	7.50	11.50	16.50	30.00	225.00
1,622,500	1841	4.50	7.00	12.00	22.50	200.00
2,007,500	1841 O	5.00	8.00	15.00	27.50	225.00
1,887,500	1842	4.50	7.00	12.00	22.50	200.00
2,020,000	1842 O	6.00	9.00	17.50	30.00	225.00
1,370,000	1843	4.50	7.00	12.00	22.50	200.00
150,000	1843 O	35.00	100.00	300.00	450.00	700.00
72,500	1844	37.50	70.00	150.00	300.00	600.00
1,755,000	1845	4.50	7.00	11.00	22.50	200.00
230,000	1845 O	35.00	75.00	150.00	350.00	750.00
31,300	1846	40.00	60.00	80.00	150.00	600.00
245,000	1847	6.50	10.00	18.50	40.00	215.00
451,500	1848	6.00	10.00	17.50	35.00	200.00
839,000	1849	4.50	7.00	15.00	35.00	200.00
300,000	1849 O	12.50	20.00	35.00	75.00	250.00
1,931,500	1850	4.50	7.00	11.00	25.00	200.00
510,000	1850 O	9.00	17.50	25.00	50.00	225.00
1,026,500	1851	4.50	7.00	11.00	30.00	200.00
400,000	1851 O	8.00	12.00	20.00	50.00	225.00
1,535,500	1852	4.50	7.00	11.00	25.00	200.00
430,000	1852 O	10.00	17.50	30.00	70.00	350.00
12,173,010††	1853	22.50	35.00	50.00	125.00	325.00

†† Includes 1853 dimes with arrows at date

With arrows at date

Quantity	Year	Good to Very Good	Fine	Very Fine	Ext. Fine	Unc.
	1853	4.50	8.00	17.50	35.00	325.00
1,100,000	1853 O	6.50	9.00	17.50	40.00	350.00
4,470,000	1854	5.00	8.00	15.00	35.00	325.00
1,770,000	1854 O	5.50	10.00	18.00	35.00	325.00
2,075,000	1855	5.00	8.00	17.00	35.00	325.00

Without arrows at date

Quantity	Year	Good to Very Good	Fine	Very Fine	Ext. Fine	Unc.
5,780,000	1856	4.50	7.50	12.00	25.00	200.00
1,180,000	1856 O	4.50	7.00	11.00	25.00	225.00
70,000	1856 S	37.50	65.00	100.00	250.00	750.00
5,580,000	1857	4.50	7.00	11.00	25.00	200.00
1,540,000	1857 O	4.50	7.50	12.50	30.00	225.00
1,540,000	1858	4.50	7.00	11.00	25.00	200.00
290,000	1858 O	6.50	10.00	17.50	45.00	250.00
60,000	1858 S	30.00	60.00	110.00	190.00	450.00
430,000	1859	4.50	7.00	12.50	25.00	200.00
480,000	1859 O	4.50	7.50	14.00	30.00	225.00
60,000	1859 S	25.00	45.00	75.00	150.00	300.00
140,000	1860 S	12.50	30.00	75.00	100.00	250.00

1860-1891

Quantity	Year	Good to Very Good	Fine	Very Fine	Ext. Fine	Unc.
607,000	1860	$4.50	$7.00	$11.00	$22.00	$125.00
40,000	1860 O rare	450.00	750.00	1000.00	1500.00	7500.00
1,924,000	1861	4.50	7.00	11.00	22.00	125.00
172,500	1861 S	16.00	30.00	50.00	100.00	275.00
847,550	1862	4.50	7.00	11.00	22.00	125.00
180,750	1862 S	12.00	30.00	45.00	65.00	275.00
14,460	1863	37.50	60.00	80.00	110.00	375.00
157,500	1863 S	20.00	35.00	60.00	90.00	300.00
39,070	1864	40.00	65.00	85.00	125.00	400.00
230,000	1864 S	12.00	25.00	35.00	55.00	300.00
10,500	1865	40.00	70.00	90.00	130.00	400.00
175,000	1865 S	12.00	30.00	60.00	90.00	300.00
8,725	1866	42.50	80.00	100.00	150.00	400.00
135,000	1866 S	12.00	30.00	55.00	85.00	300.00
6,625	1867	50.00	85.00	110.00	160.00	400.00
140,000	1867 S	12.00	30.00	50.00	85.00	300.00
466,250	1868	4.50	8.00	15.00	25.00	125.00
260,000	1868 S	10.00	20.00	35.00	55.00	175.00
256,600	1869	4.50	7.00	12.00	22.50	125.00
450,000	1869 S	9.00	17.50	25.00	45.00	175.00
471,500	1870	4.50	7.00	11.00	25.00	125.00
50,000	1870 S	65.00	100.00	140.00	250.00	425.00
753,610	1871	4.50	7.00	11.00	22.50	125.00
320,000	1871 S	12.00	25.00	40.00	75.00	325.00
20,100	1871 CC rare	200.00	350.00	550.00	1000.00	2000.00
2,396,450	1872	4.50	7.00	11.00	22.50	125.00
190,000	1872 S	12.00	25.00	40.00	65.00	150.00
24,000	1872 CC	110.00	190.00	325.00	550.00	1500.00
3,947,100	1873 no arrows	4.50	7.00	11.00	22.50	125.00
	1873 arrows	11.50	20.00	35.00	60.00	450.00
455,000	1873 S arrows	17.50	35.00	55.00	75.00	450.00
31,191	1873 CC arrows	350.00	600.00	850.00	1250.00	25,000.00
	1873 CC no arrows					(unique)
2,940,700	1874 arrows	11.00	25.00	35.00	60.00	400.00
240,000	1874 S arrows	20.00	35.00	55.00	85.00	450.00
10,817	1874 CC arrows (very rare)	100.00	200.00	400.00	1000.00	2500.00

Without arrows at date

Quantity	Year	Good to Very Good	Fine	Very Fine	Ext. Fine	Unc.
10,350,700	1875	4.50	7.00	11.00	20.00	125.00
9,070,000	1875 S in wreath	4.50	7.00	11.00	20.00	125.00
	1875 S below wreath	4.50	7.00	11.00	20.00	125.00
4,645,000	1875 CC in wreath	4.50	7.00	11.00	20.00	135.00
	1875 CC below wreath	4.50	7.50	12.50	22.50	145.00

DIMES — LIBERTY SEATED TYPE (continued)

Quantity	Year	Good to Very Good	Fine	Very Fine	Ext. Fine	Unc.

Without arrows at date

Quantity	Year	Good to Very Good	Fine	Very Fine	Ext. Fine	Unc.
11,461,150	1876	$4.50	$7.00	$10.00	$20.00	$125.00
10,420,000	1876 S	4.50	7.00	10.00	20.00	125.00
8,270,000	1876 CC	4.50	7.00	10.00	20.00	150.00
7,310,510	1877	4.50	7.00	10.00	20.00	125.00
2,340,000	1877 S	4.50	7.00	10.00	20.00	125.00
7,700,000	1877 CC	4.50	7.50	12.50	22.50	155.00
1,678,800	1878	4.50	7.00	10.00	22.00	125.00
200,000	1878 CC	17.50	27.50	40.00	60.00	175.00
15,100	1879	35.00	60.00	80.00	110.00	300.00
37,355	1880	27.50	45.00	60.00	85.00	275.00
24,975	1881	30.00	50.00	70.00	95.00	275.00
3,911,100	1882	4.50	7.00	10.00	20.00	140.00
7,675,712	1883	4.50	7.00	10.00	20.00	140.00
3,366,380	1884	4.50	7.00	10.00	20.00	140.00
564,969	1884 S	9.50	15.00	25.00	45.00	175.00
2,533,427	1885	4.50	7.00	10.00	20.00	140.00
43,690	1885 S	85.00	145.00	200.00	400.00	650.00
6,377,570	1886	4.50	7.00	10.00	20.00	125.00
206,524	1886 S	9.00	16.00	27.50	40.00	175.00
11,283,939	1887	4.50	7.00	10.00	20.00	125.00
4,454,450	1887 S	4.50	7.00	10.00	20.00	145.00
5,496,487	1888	4.50	7.00	10.00	20.00	125.00
1,720,000	1888 S	4.50	7.00	12.00	22.50	135.00
7,380,711	1889	4.50	7.00	10.00	20.00	125.00
972,678	1889 S	9.50	17.50	40.00	65.00	200.00
9,911,541	1890	4.50	7.00	10.00	20.00	125.00
1,423,076	1890 S	4.50	7.00	12.50	22.50	145.00
15,310,600	1891	4.50	7.00	10.00	20.00	125.00
4,540,000	1891 O	4.50	7.00	12.00	25.00	150.00
3,196,116	1891 S	4.50	7.00	10.00	20.00	150.00

DIMES — LIBERTY HEAD TYPE

The mint marks are under the wreath on the reverse.

Quantity	Year	Good	Very Good	Fine	Very Fine	Ext. Fine	Unc.	Proof
12,121,245	1892	$1.75	$3.25	$5.50	$8.00	$14.00	$65.00	$200.00
3,841,700	1892 O	3.75	5.00	7.50	10.50	20.00	70.00	
990,710	1892 S	19.00	27.50	32.50	45.00	65.00	140.00	
3,340,792	1893	3.50	5.00	7.50	10.00	14.00	65.00	200.00
1,760,000	1893 O	10.00	12.00	20.00	28.00	37.50	85.00	
2,491,401	1893 S	4.50	6.50	12.00	17.50	27.50	85.00	
1,330,972	1894	6.00	9.00	13.50	20.00	25.00	75.00	200.00
720,000	1894 O	25.00	40.00	65.00	85.00	130.00	350.00	
24	1894 S ext. rare						50,000.00	
690,880	1895	30.00	40.00	65.00	85.00	125.00	300.00	400.00
440,000	1895 O	60.00	80.00	130.00	180.00	275.00	850.00	
1,120,000	1895 S	12.50	17.50	22.00	35.00	50.00	185.00	
2,000,762	1896	4.00	6.75	11.00	17.50	22.00	75.00	200.00
610,000	1896 O	30.00	40.00	65.00	85.00	120.00	275.00	

DIMES — LIBERTY HEAD TYPE (continued)

Quantity	Year	Good	Very Good	Fine	Very Fine	Ext. Fine	Unc.	Proof
575,056	1896 S	$28.50	$40.00	$62.50	$87.50	$135.00	$330.00	
10,869,264	1897	1.35	2.00	4.00	7.00	12.00	65.00	$200.00
666,000	1897 O	25.00	32.50	55.00	70.00	100.00	225.00	
1,342,844	1897 S	7.00	12.00	18.50	33.00	50.00	120.00	
16,320,735	1898	1.25	1.75	3.50	6.50	12.50	65.00	200.00
2,130,000	1898 O	3.50	6.00	11.00	22.50	45.00	100.00	
1,702,507	1898 S	3.50	6.00	10.00	18.00	40.00	85.00	
19,580,846	1899	1.15	1.50	3.50	6.50	12.50	65.00	200.00
2,650,000	1899 O	3.50	5.50	11.00	20.00	40.00	95.00	
1,867,493	1899 S	3.75	6.00	10.00	16.50	30.00	90.00	
17,600,912	1900	1.15	1.50	3.00	6.50	12.50	65.00	200.00
2,010,000	1900 O	5.00	7.50	12.50	22.50	45.00	100.00	
5,168,270	1900 S	1.75	3.00	5.00	8.50	15.00	65.00	
18,860,478	1901	1.00	1.25	3.00	6.00	12.00	65.00	200.00
5,620,000	1901 O	1.60	3.00	6.50	13.50	37.50	125.00	
593,022	1901 S	21.50	40.00	75.00	110.00	175.00	600.00	
21,380,777	1902	1.00	1.25	3.00	6.00	12.00	65.00	200.00
4,500,000	1902 O	1.35	2.50	6.00	11.00	22.50	70.00	
2,070,000	1902 S	3.25	5.50	10.00	20.00	40.00	95.00	
19,500,755	1903	1.00	1.25	3.00	6.00	12.00	65.00	200.00
8,180,000	1903 O	1.25	2.50	5.00	8.50	17.50	75.00	
613,300	1903 S	20.00	25.00	37.50	55.00	90.00	275.00	
14,601,027	1904	1.00	1.25	3.00	6.00	12.00	65.00	200.00
800,000	1904 S	12.00	16.50	25.00	35.00	50.00	250.00	
14,552,350	1905	1.00	1.25	3.00	6.00	12.00	65.00	200.00
3,400,000	1905 O	1.50	2.75	6.50	11.00	20.00	80.00	
6,855,199	1905 S	1.25	2.25	4.50	8.50	15.00	75.00	
19,958,406	1906	1.00	1.25	2.50	5.00	11.00	65.00	200.00
4,060,000	1906 D	1.25	2.00	5.00	8.00	15.00	65.00	
2,610,000	1906 O	2.50	4.50	8.50	12.50	20.00	75.00	
3,136,640	1906 S	1.50	2.25	5.00	8.50	15.00	65.00	
22,220,575	1907	1.00	1.25	2.50	5.00	11.00	65.00	200.00
4,080,000	1907 D	1.25	2.00	5.00	8.00	15.00	65.00	
5,058,000	1907 O	1.25	2.00	5.00	8.00	15.00	65.00	
3,178,470	1907 S	1.25	2.00	5.00	8.00	15.00	65.00	
10,600,545	1908	.95	1.25	2.50	5.00	15.00	65.00	200.00
7,490,000	1908 D	1.00	1.50	2.50	5.00	11.00	65.00	
1,789,000	1908 O	2.75	5.00	10.00	13.00	22.50	80.00	
3,220,000	1908 S	1.25	2.25	5.00	8.00	15.00	75.00	
10,240,650	1909	.95	1.25	2.50	5.00	11.00	65.00	200.00
954,000	1909 D	3.50	5.00	12.50	22.50	35.00	110.00	
2,287,000	1909 O	2.25	3.50	7.50	12.50	22.50	90.00	
1,000,000	1909 S	4.00	6.50	15.00	25.00	37.50	100.00	
11,520,551	1910	.95	1.25	2.50	5.00	11.00	65.00	200.00
3,490,000	1910 D	1.25	1.75	4.00	6.50	15.00	65.00	
1,240,000	1910 S	2.25	3.00	6.00	11.00	22.50	90.00	
18,870,543	1911	.95	1.25	2.50	5.00	11.00	65.00	200.00
11,209,000	1911 D	1.00	1.25	2.50	5.00	11.00	65.00	
3,520,000	1911 S	1.25	1.75	3.50	7.50	15.00	65.00	
19,350,700	1912	.95	1.25	2.50	5.00	11.00	65.00	200.00
11,760,000	1912 D	1.00	1.25	2.50	5.00	11.00	65.00	
3,420,000	1912 S	1.50	2.25	4.00	7.50	15.00	65.00	
19,760,622	1913	.95	1.25	2.50	5.00	11.00	65.00	225.00
510,000	1913 S	7.00	12.50	25.00	40.00	75.00	300.00	
17,360,655	1914	.95	1.25	2.50	5.00	11.00	65.00	250.00
11,908,000	1914 D	1.00	1.25	2.50	5.00	11.00	65.00	
2,100,000	1914 S	1.50	2.25	4.25	8.50	15.00	85.00	
5,620,450	1915	.95	1.25	2.50	5.00	11.00	65.00	250.00
960,000	1915 S	2.00	2.75	5.50	10.00	17.50	90.00	
18,490,000	1916	.95	1.25	2.50	5.00	11.00	65.00	
5,820,000	1916 S	.95	1.25	2.50	5.00	11.00	65.00	

The mint marks are to the left of the fasces on the reverse.

Quantity	Year	Good	Very Good	Fine	Very Fine	Ext. Fine	Unc.
22,180,080	1916	$ .75	$1.00	$1.50	$2.00	$5.00	$20.00
264,000	1916 D	110.00	150.00	225.00	300.00	420.00	1250.00
10,450,000	1916 S	1.75	2.75	4.75	6.00	9.50	30.00
55,230,000	1917	.65	1.00	1.50	1.75	3.50	20.00
9,402,000	1917 D	2.00	4.00	7.00	10.00	20.00	85.00
27,330,000	1917 S	.75	1.25	1.75	3.00	6.50	35.00
26,680,000	1918	.75	1.25	3.25	7.00	18.00	45.00
22,674,800	1918 D	.80	1.25	4.00	6.00	15.00	65.00
19,300,000	1918 S	.75	1.25	2.25	5.00	15.00	60.00
35,740,000	1919	.65	1.10	1.50	3.00	7.00	40.00
9,939,000	1919 D	1.50	2.75	7.50	13.50	30.00	180.00
8,850,000	1919 S	1.50	3.00	7.50	13.50	30.00	190.00
59,030,000	1920	.65	1.00	1.25	1.50	3.50	25.00
19,171,000	1920 D	.75	1.50	2.00	4.00	8.50	65.00
13,820,000	1920 S	.75	1.00	1.75	3.50	9.00	65.00
1,230,000	1921	13.00	20.00	45.00	75.00	250.00	1100.00
1,080,000	1921 D	20.00	30.00	55.00	100.00	260.00	1000.00
50,130,000	1923	.60	.85	1.00	1.25	3.00	20.00
6,440,000	1923 S	.85	1.25	3.50	6.00	20.00	120.00
24,010,000	1924	.60	.85	1.00	1.50	4.00	35.00
6,810,000	1924 D	.85	1.50	3.25	5.00	15.00	150.00
7,120,000	1924 S	.75	1.15	2.25	5.00	15.00	150.00
25,610,000	1925	.65	1.00	1.25	1.50	4.00	40.00
5,117,000	1925 D	2.00	4.00	8.50	18.50	60.00	300.00
5,850,000	1925 S	.75	1.25	1.75	5.75	20.00	155.00
32,160,000	1926	.60	.85	1.00	1.25	2.75	20.00
6,828,000	1926 D	.75	1.35	2.25	4.50	12.50	80.00
1,520,000	1926 S	5.50	7.50	15.00	17.50	55.00	550.00
28,080,000	1927	.65	.90	1.00	1.25	3.00	20.00
4,812,000	1927 D	1.00	2.50	5.00	17.50	32.50	275.00
4,770,000	1927 S	.75	1.10	1.75	5.00	15.00	165.00
19,480,000	1928	.65	.90	1.00	1.25	3.00	20.00
4,161,000	1928 D	1.00	2.00	3.75	11.00	27.50	145.00
7,400,000	1928 S	.70	1.10	1.25	3.50	9.00	75.00
25,970,000	1929	.60	.90	1.00	1.25	2.50	20.00
5,034,000	1929 D	.75	1.10	2.25	3.00	4.75	22.50
4,730,000	1929 S	.70	1.00	1.50	2.50	3.75	25.00
6,770,000	1930	.70	1.00	1.25	1.50	4.00	30.00
1,843,000	1930 S	2.00	2.50	3.00	4.50	9.50	85.00
3,150,000	1931	.80	1.10	1.50	3.00	6.00	45.00
1,260,000	1931 D	5.50	6.00	8.50	13.00	20.00	75.00
1,800,000	1931 S	2.00	2.75	3.00	4.25	10.00	90.00
24,080,000	1934	.60	.90	1.10	1.20	2.25	18.50
6,772,000	1934 D	.70	1.15	1.25	1.50	5.00	37.50

Quantity	Year	Good	Very Good	Fine	Very Fine	Ext. Fine	Unc.
58,830,000	1935	$ .60	$ .90	$1.00	$1.10	$ 1.50	$ 6.00
10,477,000	1935 D	.65	1.00	1.10	1.50	5.00	65.00
15,840,000	1935 S	.65	.90	1.00	1.15	2.00	15.00
87,504,130	1936				.75	1.00	4.50
16,132,000	1936 D				1.25	4.50	32.50
9,210,000	1936 S				1.00	2.50	22.50
56,865,756	1937				.75	1.00	4.00
14,146,000	1937 D				.85	1.25	17.50
9,740,000	1937 S				.85	1.25	15.75
22,198,728	1938				.75	1.00	6.00
5,537,000	1938 D				1.00	2.00	12.50
8,090,000	1938 S				1.00	2.00	11.00
67,749,321	1939				.75	1.00	4.00
24,394,000	1939 D				.75	1.00	6.00
10,540,000	1939 S				1.25	2.50	15.00
65,361,827	1940				.75	1.00	3.00
21,198,000	1940 D				.75	1.00	9.00
21,560,000	1940 S				.75	1.00	6.00
175,106,557	1941				.75	1.00	3.00
45,634,000	1941 D				.75	1.00	4.50
43,090,000	1941 S				.75	1.00	6.50

The 1942/41 dime very clearly shows the numeral "1" at the front edge of the "2" in the date. The second "1" is close to the "4" as on the regular 1941 dimes.

Quantity	Year			Very Fine	Ext. Fine	Unc.
205,432,329 {	1942 over 1			175.00	225.00	300.00
	1942					3.00
60,740,000	1942 D			.75	1.00	4.00
49,300,000	1942 S			.75	1.00	5.00
191,710,000	1943			.75	1.00	3.00
71,949,000	1943 D			.75	1.00	3.00
60,400,000	1943 S			.75	1.00	3.00
231,410,000	1944			.75	1.00	3.00
62,224,000	1944 D			.75	1.00	3.00
49,490,000	1944 S			.75	1.00	3.00
159,130,000	1945			.75	1.00	3.00
40,245,000	1945 D			.75	1.00	3.50
41,920,000	1945 S			.75	1.00	3.00

The mint marks are at the left bottom of the torch on the reverse.

Quantity	Year	Ext. Fine	Unc.
255,250,000	1946	$ .50	$ .85
61,043,500	1946 D	.50	1.00
27,900,000	1946 S	.50	1.50
121,520,000	1947	.50	1.35
46,835,000	1947 D	.50	2.20
38,840,000	1947 S	.50	2.00
74,950,000	1948		2.00
52,841,000	1948 D		1.50
35,520,000	1948 S		1.75
30,940,000	1949		11.00
26,034,000	1949 D		6.50
13,510,000	1949 S		16.50
50,181,500	1950		2.75
46,803,000	1950 D		1.75
20,440,000	1950 S		9.50
103,937,602	1951		2.00
52,191,800	1951 D		1.25
31,630,000	1951 S		9.00
99,122,073	1952		1.00
122,100,000	1952 D		1.00
44,419,500	1952 S		3.50
53,618,920	1953		.85
136,400,000	1953 D		.80
39,180,000	1953 S		.90
114,243,503	1954		.80
106,397,000	1954 D		.80
22,860,000	1954 S		1.00
12,828,381	1955		1.50
13,959,000	1955 D		1.35
18,510,000	1955 S		1.00
108,821,081	1956		.60
108,015,100	1956 D		.60
160,160,000	1957		.60
113,354,330	1957 D		.60
31,910,000	1958		.75
136,564,600	1958 D		.60
85,780,000	1959		.60
164,919,790	1959 D		.60
70,390,000	1960		.60
200,160,400	1960 D		.60
96,758,244	1961		.60
209,146,550	1961 D		.60
75,668,019	1962		.60
334,948,380	1962 D		.60
126,725,645	1963		.60
421,476,530	1963 D		.60
929,360,000	1964		.55
1,357,517,180	1964 D		.55

		Unc.
1,649,780,570	1965	$ .20
1,380,474,957	1966	.20
2,244,007,320	1967	.20
424,470,400	1968	.20
480,748,280	1968 D	.20
3,041,509	1968 S (proof only)	
145,790,000	1969	.20
563,323,870	1969 D	.20
2,934,631	1969 S (proof only)	
345,570,000	1970	.20
754,942,100	1970 D	.20
2,632,810	1970 S (proof only)	
162,690,000	1971	.20
377,914,240	1971 D	.20
3,244,138	1971 S (proof only)	
431,540,000	1972	.20
330,290,000	1972 D	.20
3,267,667	1972 S (proof only)	
315,670,000	1973	.20
455,032,426	1973 D	.20
2,769,624	1973 S (proof only)	
470,248,000	1974	.20
571,083,000	1974 D	.20
2,617,350	1974 S (proof only)	
	1975	
	1975 D	
	1975 S (proof only)	

Twenty Cents

These silver coins were issued for a very short time, from 1875 to 1878. The difference between this coin and the popular quarter was too slight to make the twenty-cent piece useful. A peculiarity of this coin is that it had a smooth edge instead of the usual corrugated edge.

TWENTY CENT PIECES

The mint marks are under the eagle on the reverse.

Quantity	Year	Good to Very Good	Fine	Very Fine	Ext. Fine	Unc.	Proof
39,700	1875	$52.50	$60.00	$85.00	$160.00	$750.00	$1200.00
1,155,000	1875 S	45.00	55.00	75.00	115.00	700.00	
133,290	1875 CC	55.00	60.00	85.00	145.00	750.00	
15,900	1876	65.00	75.00	110.00	185.00	800.00	1225.00
10,000	1876 CC (extremely rare)						
510	1877 only proofs were struck						1400.00
600	1878 only proofs were struck						1350.00

Quarters

QUARTERS — DRAPED BUST TYPE

1796   1804-1807

Quantity	Year	Fair to Good	Very Good	Fine	Very Fine
5,894	1796 rare	$750.00	$1500.00	$2400.00	$3700.00
6,738	1804	140.00	220.00	375.00	1000.00
121,394	1805	75.00	100.00	150.00	210.00
206,124 {	1806 over 5	60.00	95.00	150.00	210.00
	1806	55.00	90.00	135.00	185.00
220,643	1807	55.00	90.00	135.00	185.00

QUARTERS — CAPPED BUST TYPE

Quantity	Year	Fair to Good	Very Good	Fine	Very Fine	Unc.
69,232	1815	$35.00	$50.00	$60.00	$145.00	$2650.00
361,174 {	1818 over 15	37.50	50.00	65.00	150.00	2650.00
	1818	35.00	50.00	60.00	140.00	2650.00
144,000	1819	35.00	50.00	60.00	95.00	2650.00
127,444	1820	35.00	55.00	60.00	95.00	2650.00
216,851	1821	35.00	50.00	55.00	95.00	2650.00
64,080 {	1822	35.00	50.00	55.00	95.00	2650.00
	1822 25 over 50c (rare)	150.00	240.00	375.00	650.00	
17,000	1823 over 22 (extremely rare)	1250.00	3500.00	7000.00	10,000.00	
?	1824	40.00	50.00	75.00	125.00	2650.00
168,000 {	1825 over 22	35.00	47.50	55.00	85.00	2650.00
	1825 over 23	35.00	47.50	55.00	85.00	2650.00
	1825 over 24	35.00	47.50	55.00	85.00	2200.00
4,000	1827 extremely rare, only a few pieces known					
102,000	1828	35.00	47.50	55.00	85.00	2650.00
?	1828 25 over 50c	60.00	100.00	175.00	285.00	3250.00

Quantity	Year	Good to Very Good	Fine	Very Fine	Ext. Fine	Unc.
398,000	1831	$37.50	$45.00	$65.00	$125.00	$1200.00
320,000	1832	37.50	45.00	65.00	125.00	1200.00
156,000	1833	37.50	50.00	85.00	200.00	1600.00
286,000	1834	37.50	45.00	65.00	125.00	1200.00
1,952,000	1835	37.50	45.00	65.00	125.00	1200.00
472,000	1836	37.50	45.00	65.00	125.00	1200.00
252,400	1837	37.50	45.00	65.00	125.00	1200.00
832,000*	1838	37.50	45.00	65.00	125.00	1200.00

QUARTERS — LIBERTY SEATED TYPE

1838-1865   1866-1891

Quantity	Year	Good to Very Good	Fine	Very Fine	Ext. Fine	Unc.
		Without drapery from elbow				
		The mint marks are under the eagle on the reverse.				
*	1838	$12.50	$20.00	$35.00	$80.00	$1250.00
491,146	1839	11.50	17.50	30.00	75.00	1250.00
425,200**	1840 O	11.50	17.50	30.00	75.00	1250.00
		With drapery from elbow				
188,127	1840	$11.00	$15.00	$30.00	$50.00	$300.00
**1840 O		8.50	14.00	22.50	37.50	325.00
120,000	1841	17.50	30.00	37.50	65.00	350.00
452,000	1841 O	9.50	14.00	22.50	35.00	300.00
88,000	1842	22.50	35.00	55.00	85.00	450.00
769,000 {	1842 O large date	10.00	14.00	25.00	40.00	350.00
	1842 O small date	16.00	25.00	40.00	60.00	350.00
645,600	1843	8.00	14.00	25.00	40.00	300.00
968,000	1843 O	8.00	14.00	25.00	40.00	300.00
421,400	1844	8.00	14.00	25.00	40.00	300.00
740,000	1844 O	8.00	14.00	25.00	40.00	350.00
922,000	1845	8.00	14.00	25.00	40.00	300.00
510,000	1846	8.00	14.00	25.00	40.00	300.00
734,000	1847	8.00	14.00	25.00	40.00	300.00
368,000	1847 O	10.00	15.00	27.50	42.50	325.00
146,000	1848	12.00	20.00	35.00	50.00	325.00
340,000	1849	10.00	15.00	27.50	42.50	300.00
?	1849 O	95.00	160.00	250.00	400.00	1000.00
190,800	1850	11.00	15.00	27.50	42.50	300.00
412,000	1850 O	12.00	20.00	35.00	50.00	350.00
160,000	1851	10.00	15.00	27.50	42.50	300.00
88,000	1851 O	35.00	60.00	90.00	150.00	850.00
177,060	1852	10.00	15.00	27.50	42.50	300.00
96,000	1852 O	50.00	100.00	175.00	300.00	1000.00
?	1853 over 52	Rare				

* includes 1838 Liberty Seated quarters.
** includes 1840 O quarters with drapery from elbow.

Quantity	Year	Good to Very Good	Fine	Very Fine	Ext. Fine	Unc.
		With arrows at date. Rays over eagle.				
15,254,220	1853	11.00	15.00	35.00	80.00	875.00
1,332,000	1853 O	11.00	20.00	35.00	100.00	1000.00
		With arrows at date. Without rays.				
12,380,000	1854	$9.50	$12.50	$20.00	$45.00	$550.00
1,484,000	1854 O	9.50	12.50	22.00	50.00	600.00
2,857,000	1855	9.50	12.50	20.00	45.00	550.00
176,000	1855 O	55.00	85.00	140.00	275.00	1000.00
396,400	1855 S	47.50	75.00	140.00	250.00	1000.00
		Without arrows at date				
7,264,000	1856	9.50	12.50	20.00	35.00	300.00
968,000	1856 O	9.50	12.50	20.00	35.00	325.00
286,000	1856 S	25.00	45.00	90.00	150.00	400.00
9,644,000	1857	9.50	12.50	20.00	35.00	300.00
1,180,000	1857 O	9.50	12.50	20.00	35.00	300.00
82,000	1857 S	35.00	60.00	100.00	175.00	500.00
7,368,000	1858	9.50	12.50	20.00	35.00	300.00
520,000	1858 O	9.50	12.50	20.00	35.00	325.00
121,000	1858 S	32.50	45.00	80.00	140.00	400.00
1,344,000	1859	9.50	12.50	20.00	35.00	300.00
260,000	1859 O	9.50	12.50	20.00	35.00	325.00
80,000	1859 S	37.50	55.00	90.00	160.00	400.00
805,400	1860	9.50	12.50	20.00	35.00	300.00
388,000	1860 O	9.50	12.50	20.00	35.00	325.00
56,000	1860 S	40.00	65.00	90.00	175.00	450.00
4,854,600	1861	9.50	12.50	20.00	35.00	300.00
96,000	1861 S	25.00	45.00	80.00	120.00	400.00
932,550	1862	9.50	12.50	20.00	35.00	300.00
67,000	1862 S	27.50	50.00	90.00	150.00	450.00

Quantity	Year	Good to Very Good	Fine	Very Fine	Ext. Fine	Unc.
192,060	1863	$11.50	$18.50	$25.00	$50.00	$350.00
94,070	1864	22.50	35.00	50.00	75.00	400.00
20,000	1864 S	50.00	90.00	150.00	225.00	750.00
59,300	1865	27.50	50.00	80.00	110.00	500.00
41,000	1865 S	32.50	55.00	90.00	125.00	550.00

With motto over eagle

Quantity	Year	Good to Very Good	Fine	Very Fine	Ext. Fine	Unc.
17,525	1866	45.00	90.00	150.00	225.00	600.00
28,005	1866 S	35.00	60.00	90.00	150.00	400.00
20,620	1867	42.00	85.00	140.00	200.00	450.00
48,000	1867 S	22.50	45.00	60.00	90.00	375.00
30,000	1868	30.00	50.00	70.00	100.00	450.00
96,000	1868 S	22.50	40.00	60.00	85.00	375.00
16,600	1869	45.00	90.00	150.00	225.00	600.00
76,000	1869 S	27.50	50.00	80.00	125.00	400.00
87,400	1870	25.00	45.00	75.00	110.00	400.00
8,340	1870 CC	150.00	245.00	375.00	650.00	1500.00
171,232	1871	9.00	15.00	20.00	40.00	250.00
30,900	1871 S	35.00	55.00	75.00	110.00	350.00
10,890	1871 CC	120.00	195.00	300.00	525.00	1500.00
182,950	1872	8.00	11.00	17.50	35.00	250.00
83,000	1872 S	22.50	40.00	65.00	100.00	350.00
9,100	1872 CC	195.00	275.00	450.00	750.00	1650.00
1,484,300*	1873 no arrows	8.50	13.50	20.00	35.00	250.00
16,462**	1873 CC no arrows	550.00	700.00	1400.00	2500.00	Rare

* includes 1873 quarters with arrows.
** includes 1873 CC quarters with arrows.

With arrows at date

Quantity	Year	Good to Very Good	Fine	Very Fine	Ext. Fine	Unc.
*	1873	20.00	27.50	55.00	95.00	450.00
156,000	1873 S	25.00	40.00	65.00	100.00	450.00
**	1873 CC	450.00	650.00	800.00	1500.00	3000.00
471,900	1874	20.00	27.50	55.00	95.00	450.00
392,000	1874 S	25.00	37.50	65.00	100.00	450.00

Without arrows at date

Quantity	Year	Good to Very Good	Fine	Very Fine	Ext. Fine	Unc.
4,293,500	1875	8.00	11.00	17.00	35.00	250.00
680,000	1875 S	9.50	16.00	27.50	45.00	250.00
140,000	1875 CC	15.00	25.00	35.00	75.00	450.00
17,817,150	1876	9.00	11.00	17.00	35.00	250.00
8,596,000	1876 S	8.00	11.00	17.00	35.00	250.00
4,944,000	1876 CC	9.00	12.50	20.00	35.00	300.00
10,911,710	1877	8.00	11.00	17.00	35.00	250.00
8,996,000	1877 S	8.00	11.00	17.00	35.00	250.00
4,192,000	1877 CC	9.00	12.50	20.00	35.00	300.00
2,260,800	1878	8.00	11.00	17.00	35.00	250.00
140,000	1878 S	150.00	250.00	350.00	475.00	850.00
996,000	1878 CC	10.00	15.00	25.00	40.00	400.00
14,700	1879	40.00	55.00	70.00	120.00	400.00
14,955	1880	40.00	55.00	70.00	120.00	400.00
12,975	1881	42.50	60.00	75.00	130.00	400.00
16,300	1882	40.00	55.00	70.00	120.00	400.00
15,439	1883	40.00	55.00	70.00	120.00	400.00
8,875	1884	50.00	65.00	85.00	150.00	475.00
14,530	1885	40.00	55.00	70.00	120.00	400.00
5,886	1886	55.00	70.00	90.00	160.00	500.00
10,710	1887	45.00	65.00	80.00	140.00	450.00
10,833	1888	45.00	65.00	80.00	140.00	450.00
1,216,000	1888 S	8.00	11.00	17.00	35.00	300.00
12,711	1889	42.50	60.00	75.00	130.00	400.00
80,590	1890	27.50	40.00	50.00	80.00	350.00
3,920,600	1891	8.00	11.00	17.00	35.00	300.00
68,000	1891 O	95.00	140.00	230.00	350.00	650.00
2,216,000	1891 S	9.00	13.00	22.50	40.00	300.00

The mint marks are under the eagle on the reverse.

Quantity	Year	Good	Very Good	Fine	Very Fine	Ext. Fine	Unc.	Proof
8,237,245	1892	$2.20	$5.00	$7.50	$17.50	$35.00	$185.00	$350.00
2,640,000	1892 O	4.50	7.00	10.00	20.00	40.00	200.00	
964,079	1892 S	12.00	16.50	27.50	37.50	65.00	250.00	
5,444,815	1893	2.25	5.00	7.50	17.50	36.00	185.00	350.00
3,396,000	1893 O	2.50	5.50	10.00	20.00	40.00	195.00	
1,454,535	1893 S	6.00	9.00	13.50	25.00	50.00	210.00	
3,432,972	1894	2.25	5.00	7.50	17.50	36.00	185.00	350.00
2,852,000	1894 O	2.75	5.50	11.00	20.00	40.00	195.00	
2,648,821	1894 S	2.25	5.50	11.00	20.00	40.00	195.00	
4,440,880	1895	2.25	4.00	7.50	17.50	36.00	185.00	350.00
2,816,000	1895 O	2.50	5.50	11.00	20.00	40.00	195.00	
1,764,681	1895 S	4.50	7.00	12.00	22.00	40.00	195.00	
3,874,762	1896	2.25	4.00	7.50	17.50	36.00	185.00	425.00
1,484,000	1896 O	4.25	7.50	17.50	30.00	60.00	375.00	
188,039	1896 S	100.00	150.00	250.00	325.00	500.00	1850.00	
8,140,731	1897	2.00	3.00	7.00	16.50	35.00	185.00	350.00
1,414,800	1897 O	6.50	10.00	17.50	27.50	50.00	350.00	
542,229	1897 S	12.00	14.00	22.50	40.00	65.00	375.00	
11,100,735	1898	2.00	3.00	7.00	16.00	35.00	185.00	350.00
1,868,000	1898 O	3.00	5.50	11.00	18.50	40.00	190.00	
1,020,592	1898 S	4.50	7.50	11.00	17.50	35.00	300.00	
12,624,846	1899	2.00	3.00	6.50	16.00	35.00	185.00	350.00
2,644,000	1899 O	2.50	4.00	8.00	17.50	35.00	200.00	
708,000	1899 S	7.00	12.00	18.00	30.00	45.00	210.00	
10,016,912	1900	2.00	3.00	7.00	16.00	35.00	185.00	350.00
3,416,000	1900 O	4.50	8.00	12.00	20.00	40.00	195.00	
1,858,585	1900 S	2.25	4.00	9.00	16.00	35.00	195.00	
8,892,813	1901	2.25	3.00	7.00	16.00	33.00	185.00	350.00
1,612,000	1901 O	9.00	14.00	30.00	55.00	95.00	350.00	
72,664	1901 S	375.00	425.00	550.00	650.00	950.00	2750.00	
12,197,744	1902	2.00	3.00	6.50	16.00	35.00	185.00	360.00
4,748,000	1902 O	2.25	3.50	10.00	17.00	35.00	195.00	
1,524,612	1902 S	6.00	9.00	14.00	25.00	45.00	280.00	
9,670,064	1903	2.25	3.50	7.00	16.00	35.00	185.00	350.00
3,500,000	1903 O	2.25	4.00	8.50	25.00	45.00	250.00	
1,036,000	1903 S	6.00	9.00	17.50	35.00	55.00	350.00	
9,588,813	1904	2.25	3.50	7.00	16.00	35.00	185.00	350.00
2,456,000	1904 O	4.75	7.50	15.00	27.50	65.00	300.00	
4,968,250	1905	2.25	3.50	7.00	16.00	35.00	185.00	350.00
1,230,000	1905 O	4.75	9.00	15.00	25.00	45.00	200.00	
1,884,000	1905 S	3.50	4.50	8.50	17.50	35.00	190.00	
3,656,435	1906	2.00	3.00	7.00	16.00	35.00	185.00	350.00
3,280,000	1906 D	2.25	3.50	8.00	17.00	35.00	190.00	
2,056,000	1906 O	3.75	5.50	9.00	20.00	35.00	190.00	
7,192,575	1907	2.00	3.00	6.50	16.00	35.00	185.00	350.00
2,484,000	1907 D	2.50	3.50	8.00	17.00	35.00	190.00	
4,560,000	1907 O	2.25	3.50	7.00	17.00	35.00	190.00	
1,360,000	1907 S	2.50	3.50	8.00	18.00	35.00	190.00	
4,232,545	1908	2.00	3.00	7.00	16.00	35.00	185.00	350.00
5,788,000	1908 D	2.00	3.00	6.00	16.00	35.00	190.00	
6,244,000	1908 O	2.00	3.00	6.00	16.00	35.00	190.00	
784,000	1908 S	6.00	9.00	15.00	22.00	40.00	300.00	

QUARTERS — LIBERTY HEAD (BARBER) TYPE (continued)

Quantity	Year	Good	Very Good	Fine	Very Fine	Ext. Fine	Unc.	Proof
9,268,650	1909	$2.00	$3.00	$6.00	$16.00	$35.00	$185.00	$350.00
5,114,000	1909 D	2.00	3.00	6.00	16.00	35.00	190.00	
712,000	1909 O	9.00	16.50	32.00	50.00	95.00	550.00	
1,348,000	1909 S	2.25	3.50	7.00	16.00	35.00	190.00	
2,244,551	1910	2.00	3.00	6.50	16.00	35.00	185.00	350.00
1,500,000	1910 D	2.25	3.50	7.50	17.50	35.00	195.00	
3,720,543	1911	2.00	3.00	6.50	16.00	35.00	185.00	350.00
933,600	1911 D	3.00	5.00	10.00	20.00	37.50	190.00	
988,000	1911 S	2.50	3.50	8.00	17.50	35.00	190.00	
4,400,700	1912	2.00	3.00	6.50	16.00	35.00	185.00	350.00
708,000	1912 S	2.50	4.00	9.00	20.00	40.00	300.00	
484,613	1913	4.50	9.00	20.00	37.50	90.00	385.00	475.00
1,450,800	1913 D	2.50	3.50	8.00	18.00	35.00	185.00	
40,000	1913 S	125.00	175.00	300.00	400.00	600.00	1800.00	
6,244,610	1914	2.00	3.00	6.00	16.00	35.00	185.00	425.00
3,046,000	1914 D	2.00	3.00	6.00	16.00	35.00	185.00	
264,000	1914 S	12.00	12.50	22.50	40.00	85.00	365.00	
3,480,450	1915	2.00	3.00	6.00	16.00	35.00	185.00	475.00
3,694,000	1915 D	2.00	3.00	6.00	16.00	35.00	190.00	
704,000	1915 S	2.50	3.50	8.50	18.00	36.00	225.00	
1,788,000	1916	2.00	3.00	6.50	16.00	35.00	185.00	
6,540,800	1916 D	2.00	3.00	6.00	16.00	35.00	190.00	

QUARTERS — STANDING LIBERTY TYPE

The mint marks are above and to the left of the date on the obverse.

1916-1917   1917-1930

Quantity	Year	Good	Very Good	Fine	Very Fine	Ext. Fine	Unc.
52,000	1916	$275.00	$325.00	$450.00	$500.00	$625.00	$1300.00
8,792,000	1917 type I*	5.50	7.00	10.00	16.00	30.00	175.00
1,509,200	1917 D type I*	5.50	8.00	12.00	17.50	35.00	200.00
1,952,000	1917 S type I*	5.50	8.00	12.00	17.50	35.00	200.00
13,880,000	1917 type II**	5.50	7.50	9.50	12.00	25.00	85.00
6,224,400	1917 Dtype II**	10.50	13.00	16.50	22.50	30.00	110.00
5,552,000	1917 S type II**	9.50	13.50	18.50	22.50	35.00	115.00
14,240,000	1918	3.75	5.50	9.50	13.00	25.00	85.00
7,380,000	1918 D	7.50	11.00	15.00	17.50	30.00	100.00
11,072,000	1918 S	4.00	6.00	10.00	15.00	25.00	95.00
?	1918 S over 17	225.00	300.00	450.00	600.00	850.00	5000.00
11,324,000	1919	6.00	10.00	14.00	20.00	27.50	90.00
1,944,000	1919 D	25.00	30.00	45.00	60.00	100.00	375.00
1,836,000	1919 S	25.00	32.50	45.00	55.00	120.00	390.00
27,860,000	1920	3.75	4.50	6.00	8.50	12.50	85.00
3,586,400	1920 D	10.00	15.00	20.00	32.50	50.00	160.00
6,380,000	1920 S	6.00	9.00	12.00	15.00	30.00	110.00

* stars at sides of eagle

** 3 stars below eagle

QUARTERS — STANDING LIBERTY TYPE (continued)

Quantity	Year	Good	Very Good	Fine	Very Fine	Ext. Fine	Unc.
1,916,000	1921	$25.00	$35.00	$50.00	$60.00	$90.00	$325.00
9,716,000	1923	3.25	5.00	7.00	8.50	17.50	85.00
1,360,000	1923 S	35.00	45.00	60.00	70.00	115.00	315.00
10,920,000	1924	3.00	4.00	6.00	8.50	17.50	85.00
3,112,000	1924 D	12.00	17.50	20.00	25.00	30.00	105.00
2,860,000	1924 S	7.00	10.00	16.00	20.00	30.00	115.00
12,280,000	1925	1.50	2.25	3.75	6.50	15.00	80.00
11,316,000	1926	1.50	2.25	3.75	6.50	15.00	80.00
1,716,000	1926 D	1.75	2.75	5.50	8.50	17.50	80.00
2,700,000	1926 S	1.75	2.75	6.00	12.50	30.00	225.00
11,912,000	1927	1.50	2.25	3.50	6.00	15.00	80.00
976,400	1927 D	2.50	4.00	8.50	12.50	25.00	110.00
396,000	1927 S	4.75	7.50	17.50	45.00	100.00	825.00
6,336,000	1928	1.50	2.25	3.50	6.00	15.00	80.00
1,627,600	1928 D	1.75	2.75	4.25	6.00	15.00	85.00
2,644,000	1928 S	1.50	2.25	3.75	6.00	15.00	85.00
11,140,000	1929	1.50	2.25	3.50	6.00	15.00	80.00
1,358,000	1929 D	1.75	2.50	4.25	6.50	17.50	95.00
1,764,000	1929 S	1.50	2.25	3.50	6.00	15.00	85.00
5,632,000	1930	1.50	2.25	3.50	6.00	15.00	80.00
1,556,000	1930 S	1.75	2.50	3.50	6.00	15.00	85.00

QUARTERS — WASHINGTON TYPE

The mint marks are under the eagle on the reverse.

Quantity	Year	Very Good	Fine	Very Fine	Ext. Fine	Unc.
5,404,000	1932	$1.50	$1.75	$2.00	$4.00	$30.00
436,800	1932 D	40.00	50.00	60.00	85.00	450.00
408,000	1932 S	40.00	45.00	50.00	65.00	190.00
31,912,052	1934	1.40	1.60	2.00	4.50	16.00
3,527,200	1934 D	2.25	5.00	7.50	17.50	80.00
32,484,000	1935	1.30	1.50	2.00	3.00	13.50
5,780,000	1935 D	1.50	2.50	5.00	10.00	85.00
5,660,000	1935 S	1.50	2.50	4.00	10.00	45.00
41,303,837	1936	1.40	1.60	2.00	2.50	14.00
5,374,000	1936 D	2.50	5.00	11.00	40.00	290.00
3,828,000	1936 S	1.50	2.50	3.50	9.00	55.00
19,701,542	1937	1.30	1.60	2.00	3.00	20.00
7,189,600	1937 D	1.50	1.75	2.75	4.50	25.00
1,652,000	1937 S	6.00	8.00	10.00	20.00	75.00
9,480,045	1938	1.50	2.00	6.00	12.00	42.50
2,832,000	1938 S	2.50	4.00	6.00	10.00	36.00
33,548,795	1939	1.40	1.75	2.00	3.00	10.00
7,092,000	1939 D	1.50	1.75	2.00	3.50	20.00
2,628,000	1939 S	2.25	3.00	4.00	10.00	37.50
35,715,246	1940	1.50	1.75	2.00	3.50	12.00
2,797,600	1940 D	2.00	3.25	6.00	12.50	45.00
8,244,000	1940 S	1.30	1.50	1.75	2.75	22.50
79,047,287	1941	1.25	1.50	1.60	2.00	5.50
16,714,800	1941 D	1.25	1.50	1.75	2.40	17.50
16,080,000	1941 S	1.25	1.50	1.75	2.25	14.00

Quantity	Year	Very Fine	Ext. Fine	Unc.
102,117,123	1942	$ .50	$1.50	$4.00
17,487,200	1942 D	1.25	2.50	22.50
19,384,000	1942 S	2.50	4.50	37.50
99,700,000	1943	.50	1.50	3.50
16,095,600	1943 D	1.25	2.50	9.00
21,700,000	1943 S	1.25	2.50	13.00
104,956,000	1944	.50	1.50	4.00
14,600,000	1944 D	.50	1.50	5.00
12,560,000	1944 S	1.25	2.50	8.00
74,372,000	1945	.50	1.50	2.25
12,341,600	1945 D	.50	1.50	5.50
17,004,001	1945 S	.50	1.50	3.50
53,436,000	1946	.50	1.50	3.25
9,072,800	1946 D	.50	1.50	7.00
4,204,000	1946 S	1.25	2.50	5.25
22,556,000	1947	.50	1.50	2.75
15,338,400	1947 D	.50	1.50	2.75
5,532,000	1947 S	1.00	2.50	4.00
35,196,000	1948	.50	1.50	2.25
16,766,800	1948 D	.50	1.50	3.00
15,960,000	1948 S	.50	1.50	2.50
9,312,000	1949	2.00	3.50	16.50
10,068,400	1949 D	1.25	2.50	7.75
24,971,512	1950	.50	1.50	2.00
21,075,600	1950 D	.50	1.50	4.00
10,284,600	1950 S	.50	1.50	5.75
43,505,602	1951	.50	1.50	2.25
35,354,800	1951 D	.50	1.50	2.75
8,948,000	1951 S	1.25	2.50	10.00
38,862,073	1952	.50	1.25	2.25
49,795,200	1952 D	.50	1.00	1.75
13,707,800	1952 S	.50	1.50	4.75
18,664,920	1953	.50	1.25	2.25
56,112,400	1953 D	.50	1.00	1.75
14,016,000	1953 S	.50	1.25	3.25
54,645,503	1954	.50	1.00	1.75
46,305,000	1954 D	.50	1.00	1.75
11,834,722	1954 S	.50	1.00	2.00
18,558,381	1955	.50	1.00	2.25
3,182,400	1955 D	1.25	2.50	5.00
44,325,081	1956		.60	1.50
32,334,500	1956 D		.60	1.50
46,720,000	1957		.60	1.50
77,924,160	1957 D		.60	1.50
6,360,000	1958		1.00	2.25
78,124,900	1958 D		.50	1.50
24,374,000	1959		.50	1.50
62,054,232	1959 D		.50	1.50
29,164,000	1960		.50	1.50
63,000,324	1960 D		.50	1.50
40,064,244	1961		.50	1.50
83,656,928	1961 D		.50	1.50
39,374,019	1962		.50	1.50
127,554,756	1962 D		.50	1.50
77,391,645	1963		.50	1.50
135,288,184	1963 D		.50	1.50
570,390,585	1964		.50	1.50
704,135,528	1964 D		.50	1.50
1,817,357,540	1965			.50
818,836,911	1966			.50
1,524,031,848	1967			.50
220,731,500	1968			.50
101,534,500	1968 D			.60
3,041,509	1968 S (proof only)			

Quantity	Year	Unc.
176,212,000	1969	$ .50
114,372,000	1969 D	.65
2,934,631	1969 S (proof only)	
136,420,000	1970	.50
417,341,364	1970 D	.50
2,632,810	1970 S (proof only)	
109,284,000	1971	.50
258,634,428	1971 D	.50
3,224,138	1971 S (proof only)	
215,048,000	1972	.50
311,067,732	1972 D	.50
3,267,667	1972 S (proof only)	
346,924,000	1973	.50
232,977,400	1973 D	.50
2,796,624	1973 S (proof only)	
*	1974	.50
*	1974 D	.50
2,617,350	1974 S (proof only)	

**	1976 Bicentennial reverse	
**	1976 D	

* Mintage continued into 1975—struck simultaneously with Bicentennial coins dated 1776–1976.
** Mintage of Bicentennial coins dated 1776–1976 began in April 1975.

Half Dollars

HALF DOLLARS — FLOWING HAIR TYPE

Quantity	Year	Good to Very Good	Fine	Very Fine
5,300	1794	$350.00	$600.00	$1250.00
317,836	1795	180.00	290.00	475.00

HALF DOLLARS — DRAPED BUST TYPE

1796-1797   1801-1807

Quantity	Year	Good to Very Good	Fine	Very Fine
?	1796 15 stars, rare	$2500.00	$4500.00	$7500.00
?	1796 16 stars, rare	2400.00	4700.00	7000.00
3,918	1797 rare	2300.00	4250.00	7000.00
30,289	1801	140.00	250.00	450.00
29,890	1802	115.00	215.00	375.00
31,715	1803	60.00	100.00	175.00
156,519	1805 over 4	75.00	125.00	225.00
211,722	1805	45.00	70.00	120.00
839,576 {	1806 over 5	55.00	85.00	160.00
	1806 over 9 (inverted 6)	85.00	135.00	260.00
	1806	45.00	80.00	150.00
301,076	1807 bust right	45.00	65.00	120.00

HALF DOLLARS — CAPPED BUST TYPE

Quantity	Year	Fine	Very Fine	Ext. Fine	Unc.
750.000 {	1807 bust left	$47.50	$85.00	$150.00	$750.00
	1807 50 over 20	42.50	80.00	115.00	750.00
1,368,600 {	1808 over 7	35.00	50.00	85.00	475.00
	1808	25.00	35.00	75.00	450.00
1,405,810	1809	25.00	35.00	70.00	425.00
1,276,276	1810	25.00	35.00	65.00	415.00
1,203,644 {	1811	25.00	35.00	75.00	425.00
	1811 as 18.11	55.00	95.00	115.00	500.00
1,628,059 {	1812 over 11	40.00	60.00	100.00	475.00
	1812	25.00	35.00	70.00	425.00
1,241,903	1813	25.00	35.00	70.00	425.00
1,039,075 {	1814 over 13	35.00	50.00	90.00	525.00
	1814	25.00	35.00	60.00	425.00
47,015	1815 over 12	400.00	500.00	600.00	2500.00

Quantity	Year	Fine	Very Fine	Ext. Fine	Unc.
1,215,567	1817 over 13	$40.00	$55.00	$95.00	$475.00
	1817	25.00	35.00	60.00	425.00
	1817 as 181.7	35.00	50.00	85.00	575.00
1,960,322	1818	25.00	35.00	45.00	425.00
	1818 over 17	25.00	35.00	45.00	500.00
2,208,000	1819 over 18	27.50	37.50	47.50	500.00
	1819	25.00	35.00	45.00	450.00
751,122	1820 over 19	30.00	37.50	60.00	525.00
	1820	30.00	40.00	60.00	550.00
1,305,797	1821	25.00	35.00	45.00	425.00
1,559,573	1822	25.00	35.00	45.00	425.00
	1822 over 21	70.00	90.00	140.00	525.00
1,694,200	1823 over 22	70.00	85.00	100.00	550.00
	1823	25.00	35.00	45.00	475.00
3,504,954	1824 over other dates	25.00	35.00	45.00	525.00
	1824 over 21	25.00	35.00	45.00	525.00
	1824	25.00	30.00	40.00	400.00
2,934,166	1825	25.00	30.00	40.00	400.00
4,004,180	1826	25.00	30.00	40.00	400.00
5,493,400	1827 over 26	25.00	35.00	55.00	450.00
	1827	25.00	30.00	50.00	450.00
3,075,200	1828	25.00	30.00	40.00	400.00
3,712,156	1829 over 27	25.00	35.00	45.00	475.00
	1829	22.50	30.00	40.00	400.00
4,764,800	1830	22.50	30.00	40.00	400.00
5,873,660	1831	22.50	30.00	40.00	400.00
4,797,000	1832	22.50	30.00	40.00	400.00
5,206,000	1833	22.50	30.00	40.00	400.00
6,412,004	1834	22.50	30.00	40.00	400.00
5,352,006	1835	22.50	30.00	40.00	400.00
6,546,200	1836 lettered edge	22.50	30.00	40.00	400.00
	1836 milled edge	150.00	375.00	900.00	2000.00
3,629,820	1837	45.00	75.00	125.00	900.00
3,546,000	1838	45.00	75.00	125.00	900.00
20	1838 O (extremely rare)				40,000.00
3,334,560*	1839	45.00	75.00	125.00	900.00
162,976	1839 O mint mark on obv.	100.00	135.00	200.00	1500.00

* includes 1839 Liberty Seated half dollars

HALF DOLLARS — LIBERTY SEATED TYPE

1839-1865   1866-1891

The mint marks are under the eagle on the reverse.

80

HALF DOLLARS — LIBERTY SEATED TYPE (continued)

Quantity	Year	Good to Very Good	Fine	Very Fine	Ext. Fine	Unc.
(see above) {	1839 no drapery	$42.50	$75.00	$125.00	$275.00	$1800.00
	1839 with drapery	13.50	25.00	40.00	70.00	375.00
1,435,008 {	1840 small letters	13.00	21.00	32.50	60.00	350.00
	1840 large letters	35.00	60.00	100.00	175.00	450.00
855,100	1840 O	13.00	21.00	35.00	60.00	350.00
310,000	1841	14.00	24.00	37.50	65.00	350.00
401,000	1841 O	13.00	21.00	35.00	60.00	350.00
2,012,764	1842	13.00	21.00	32.50	55.00	350.00
?	1842 O small date (rare)	75.00	125.00	250.00	550.00	Rare
957,000	1842 O large date	13.00	21.00	32.50	60.00	350.00
3,844,000	1843	13.00	21.00	32.50	60.00	350.00
2,268,000	1843 O	13.00	21.00	32.50	60.00	350.00
1,766,000	1844	13.00	21.00	32.50	60.00	350.00
2,005,000	1844 O	13.00	21.00	32.50	60.00	350.00
589,000	1845	14.00	22.50	35.00	65.00	350.00
2,094,000	1845 O	13.00	21.00	32.50	60.00	350.00
2,210,000 {	1846 horizontal 6 error	50.00	85.00	135.00	175.00	500.00
	1846	13.00	21.00	32.50	60.00	350.00
2,304,000 {	1846 O small date	13.00	21.00	32.50	60.00	350.00
	1846 O large date	35.00	65.00	115.00	145.00	475.00
1,156,000 {	1847 over 46	450.00	750.00	1250.00	2000.00	Rare
	1847	13.00	21.00	32.50	60.00	350.00
2,584,000	1847 O	13.00	21.00	32.50	60.00	350.00
580,000	1848	13.00	21.00	32.50	60.00	350.00
3,180,000	1848 O	13.00	21.00	32.50	60.00	350.00
1,252,000	1849	13.00	21.00	32.50	60.00	350.00
2,310,000	1849 O	13.00	21.00	32.50	60.00	350.00
227,000	1850	32.50	50.00	80.00	125.00	450.00
2,456,000	1850 O	13.00	21.00	35.00	60.00	400.00
200,750	1851	20.00	50.00	80.00	115.00	500.00
402,000	1851 O	16.50	25.00	40.00	75.00	375.00
77,130	1852	35.00	75.00	150.00	225.00	700.00
144,000	1852 O	27.50	45.00	75.00	125.00	500.00
?	1853 O no arrows (extremely rare)					
3,532,708	1853 arrows	15.00	35.00	75.00	175.00	2000.00
1,328,000	1853 O arrows	15.00	35.00	75.00	175.00	2000.00
2,982,000	1854	12.00	20.00	30.00	65.00	525.00
5,240,000	1854 O	12.00	20.00	30.00	65.00	525.00
759,500	1855	12.00	20.00	30.00	70.00	525.00
3,688,000	1855 O	12.00	20.00	30.00	70.00	575.00
129,950	1855 S rare	55.00	110.00	200.00	300.00	1000.00
938,000	1856	12.00	20.00	30.00	55.00	350.00
2,658,000	1856 O	12.00	20.00	30.00	55.00	350.00
211,000	1856 S	18.00	30.00	75.00	110.00	475.00
1,988,000	1857	12.00	20.00	30.00	55.00	350.00
818,000	1857 O	12.00	20.00	30.00	55.00	350.00
158,000	1857 S	23.00	40.00	80.00	125.00	500.00
4,226,000	1858	12.00	20.00	30.00	55.00	350.00
7,294,000	1858 O	12.00	20.00	30.00	55.00	350.00
476,000	1858 S	15.00	27.50	37.50	80.00	475.00
748,000	1859	12.00	20.00	30.00	55.00	350.00
2,834,000	1859 O	12.00	20.00	30.00	55.00	350.00
566,000	1859 S	13.50	25.00	37.50	70.00	450.00
303,700	1860	12.00	20.00	30.00	55.00	350.00
1,290,000	1860 O	12.00	20.00	30.00	55.00	350.00
472,000	1860 S	13.50	22.50	35.00	60.00	375.00
2,888,400	1861	12.00	20.00	30.00	55.00	350.00
2,532,633*	1861 O	12.00	20.00	30.00	55.00	350.00
939,500	1861 S	12.00	20.00	30.00	55.00	350.00

* All but 300,000 of these coins were struck after the Confederate forces seized the New Orleans Mint.

Quantity	Year	Good to Very Good	Fine	Very Fine	Ext. Fine	Unc.
252,350	1862	$14.00	$22.50	$32.50	$60.00	$350.00
1,352,000	1862 S	12.00	20.00	30.00	55.00	350.00
503,660	1863	12.00	20.00	30.00	55.00	350.00
916,000	1863 S	12.00	20.00	30.00	55.00	350.00
379,570	1864	12.00	20.00	30.00	55.00	350.00
658,000	1864 S	12.00	20.00	30.00	55.00	350.00
511,900	1865	12.00	20.00	30.00	55.00	350.00
675,000	1865 S	12.00	20.00	30.00	55.00	350.00
745,625	1866 motto	11.00	18.00	27.50	47.50	300.00
1,054,000 {	1866 S no motto	60.00	100.00	200.00	265.00	650.00
	1866 S motto	11.00	18.00	27.50	47.50	300.00
424,325	1867	11.00	18.00	27.50	47.50	300.00
1,196,000	1867 S	11.00	18.00	27.50	47.50	300.00
378,200	1868	11.00	18.00	27.50	47.50	300.00
1,160,000	1868 S	11.00	18.00	27.50	47.50	300.00
795,900	1869	11.00	18.00	27.50	47.50	300.00
656,000	1869 S	11.00	18.00	27.50	47.50	300.00
600,900	1870	11.00	18.00	27.50	47.50	300.00
1,004,000	1870 S	11.00	18.00	27.50	47.50	300.00
54,617	1870 CC	65.00	115.00	225.00	450.00	1200.00
1,165,350	1871	11.00	18.00	27.50	27.50	300.00
2,178,000	1871 S	11.00	18.00	27.50	47.50	300.00
139,950	1871 CC	50.00	100.00	200.00	400.00	3000.00
881,550	1872	11.00	18.00	27.50	47.50	300.00
580,000	1872 S	11.00	18.00	27.50	47.50	300.00
272,000	1872 CC	40.00	75.00	125.00	250.00	750.00
2,617,500 {	1873 no arrows	11.00	18.00	27.50	47.50	300.00
	1873 arrows	22.00	40.00	75.00	125.00	550.00
337,060 {	1873 CC no arrows	45.00	100.00	150.00	210.00	1600.00
	1873 CC arrows	40.00	100.00	140.00	200.00	1500.00
233,000	1873 S	27.50	47.50	85.00	140.00	550.00
2,360,300	1874	22.00	40.00	75.00	125.00	550.00
394,000	1874 S	30.00	60.00	85.00	150.00	550.00
59,000	1874 CC	50.00	110.00	185.00	265.00	1000.00
6,027,500	1875	11.00	18.00	27.50	47.50	300.00
3,200,000	1875 S	11.00	18.00	27.50	47.50	300.00
1,008,000	1875 CC	14.00	22.50	35.00	55.00	400.00
8,419,150	1876	11.00	18.00	27.50	47.50	300.00
4,528,000	1876 S	11.00	18.00	27.50	47.50	300.00
1,956,000	1876 CC	14.00	22.50	35.00	55.00	350.00
8,304,510	1877	11.00	18.00	27.50	47.50	300.00
5,356,000	1877 S	11.00	18.00	27.50	47.50	300.00
1,420,000	1877 CC	14.00	22.50	35.00	55.00	350.00
1,378,400	1878	11.00	18.00	27.50	47.50	300.00
12,000	1878 S	500.00	1400.00	2000.00	4000.00	12000.00
62,000	1878 CC	100.00	150.00	250.00	450.00	800.00
5,900	1879	75.00	90.00	120.00	150.00	500.00
9,755	1880	67.50	80.00	100.00	125.00	450.00
10,975	1881	67.50	80.00	100.00	125.00	450.00
5,500	1882	75.00	90.00	120.00	150.00	500.00
9,039	1883	67.50	80.00	100.00	125.00	450.00
5,275	1884	75.00	90.00	120.00	150.00	500.00
6,130	1885	75.00	90.00	120.00	150.00	500.00
5,886	1886	80.00	100.00	130.00	165.00	500.00
5,710	1887	75.00	90.00	120.00	150.00	500.00
12,833	1888	67.50	80.00	100.00	125.00	450.00
12,711	1889	67.50	80.00	100.00	125.00	450.00
12,590	1890	67.50	80.00	100.00	125.00	450.00
200,600	1891	12.50	20.00	30.00	50.00	350.00

The mint marks are under the eagle on the reverse.

Quantity	Year	Good	Very Good	Fine	Very Fine	Ext. Fine	Unc.	Proof
935,245	1892	$7.50	$12.00	$25.00	$40.00	$110.00	$420.00	$525.00
390,000	1892 O	60.00	70.00	85.00	115.00	170.00	450.00	
1,029,028	1892 S	50.00	65.00	80.00	100.00	140.00	475.00	
1,826,792	1893	7.50	12.00	25.00	40.00	110.00	400.00	525.00
1,389,000	1893 O	14.00	22.50	30.00	50.00	110.00	450.00	
740,000	1893 S	35.00	55.00	75.00	100.00	150.00	475.00	
1,148,972	1894	7.50	12.00	25.00	40.00	110.00	400.00	525.00
2,138,000	1894 O	7.50	12.00	28.00	42.50	110.00	425.00	
4,048,690	1894 S	5.00	7.00	23.00	37.50	110.00	420.00	
1,835,218	1895	5.00	7.50	24.00	37.50	100.00	400.00	525.00
1,766,000	1895 O	7.50	12.00	25.00	40.00	110.00	430.00	
1,108,086	1895 S	13.00	20.00	32.00	50.00	110.00	430.00	
950,762	1896	6.00	10.00	25.00	40.00	110.00	430.00	525.00
924,000	1896 O	13.50	18.00	30.00	55.00	125.00	425.00	
1,140,948	1896 S	33.00	45.00	65.00	90.00	135.00	450.00	
2,480,731	1897	5.00	6.00	15.00	33.00	100.00	400.00	525.00
632,000	1897 O	35.00	45.00	65.00	90.00	160.00	525.00	
933,900	1897 S	35.00	50.00	70.00	95.00	160.00	575.00	
2,956,735	1898	5.00	6.00	12.00	33.00	100.00	400.00	525.00
874,000	1898 O	9.00	14.00	25.00	42.50	110.00	420.00	
2,358,550	1898 S	6.00	8.00	16.00	40.00	100.00	400.00	
5,538,846	1899	4.75	5.50	12.00	33.00	100.00	400.00	525.00
1,724,000	1899 O	5.00	6.00	15.00	35.00	100.00	420.00	
1,686,411	1899 S	8.00	12.00	20.00	40.00	100.00	420.00	
4,762,912	1900	4.50	5.00	10.00	33.00	100.00	400.00	525.00
2,744,000	1900 O	4.50	5.50	11.00	33.00	100.00	420.00	
2,560,322	1900 S	5.50	7.00	11.00	33.00	100.00	400.00	
4,268,813	1901	4.50	5.00	10.00	33.00	100.00	400.00	525.00
1,124,000	1901 O	5.00	8.00	18.00	50.00	125.00	425.00	
847,044	1901 S	10.00	17.50	45.00	100.00	215.00	1100.00	
4,922,777	1902	4.50	5.00	10.00	33.00	100.00	400.00	525.00
2,526,000	1902 O	5.00	5.50	11.00	33.00	100.00	420.00	
1,460,670	1902 S	5.00	6.00	13.50	37.00	100.00	425.00	
2,278,755	1903	5.00	5.50	20.00	33.00	100.00	400.00	525.00
2,100,000	1903 O	5.00	5.50	12.50	33.00	100.00	400.00	
1,920,772	1903 S	4.50	6.00	17.50	37.00	100.00	475.00	
2,992,670	1904	4.50	5.00	10.00	33.00	100.00	400.00	525.00
1,117,600	1904 O	5.00	7.00	13.00	37.00	110.00	400.00	
553,038	1904 S	9.50	17.50	33.00	60.00	125.00	500.00	
662,727	1905	5.00	9.00	20.00	42.50	110.00	495.00	525.00
505,000	1905 O	8.00	15.00	30.00	52.00	125.00	425.00	
2,494,000	1905 S	4.50	5.00	10.00	32.00	100.00	400.00	

HALF DOLLARS — LIBERTY HEAD (BARBER) TYPE (continued)

Quantity	Year	Good	Very Good	Fine	Very Fine	Ext. Fine	Unc.	Proof
2,638,675	1906	$4.50	$5.00	$10.00	$32.00	$100.00	$400.00	$525.00
4,028,000	1906 D	4.50	5.00	10.00	32.00	100.00	400.00	
2,446,000	1906 O	4.50	5.00	10.00	32.00	100.00	400.00	
1,740,154	1906 S	5.00	5.50	11.00	32.50	100.00	400.00	
2,598,575	1907	4.50	5.00	10.00	32.00	100.00	400.00	525.00
3,856,000	1907 D	4.50	5.00	10.00	32.00	100.00	400.00	
3,946,600	1907 O	4.50	5.00	10.00	32.00	100.00	400.00	
1.250,000	1907 S	4.50	5.00	11.00	32.50	100.00	400.00	
1,354,545	1908	4.50	5.00	11.00	32.50	100.00	400.00	525.00
3,280,000	1908 D	4.50	5.00	10.00	32.00	100.00	400.00	
5,360,000	1908 O	4.50	5.00	10.00	32.00	100.00	400.00	
1,644,828	1908 S	4.50	5.00	11.00	32.00	100.00	400.00	
2,368,650	1909	4.50	5.00	10.00	32.00	100.00	400.00	525.00
925,400	1909 O	4.50	5.50	11.00	32.00	100.00	500.00	
1,764,000	1909 S	4.50	5.00	10.00	32.00	100.00	400.00	
418,551	1910	6.50	10.50	16.00	40.00	110.00	475.00	550.00
1,948,000	1910 S	4.50	5.00	10.00	32.00	100.00	400.00	
1,406,543	1911	4.50	5.00	10.00	32.00	100.00	400.00	525.00
695,080	1911 D	4.50	5.00	12.00	35.00	100.00	425.00	
1,272,000	1911 S	4.50	5.00	10.00	32.00	100.00	400.00	
1,550,700	1912	4.50	5.00	10.00	32.00	100.00	400.00	525.00
2,300,800	1912 D	4.50	5.00	10.00	32.00	100.00	400.00	
1,370,000	1912 S	4.50	5.00	10.00	32.00	100.00	400.00	
188,627	1913	13.50	18.50	32.50	47.50	110.00	550.00	600.00
534,000	1913 D	4.50	6.00	11.00	37.50	100.00	425.00	
604,000	1913 S	4.50	5.50	12.00	35.00	100.00	425.00	
124,610	1914	20.00	27.50	45.00	65.00	135.00	600.00	700.00
992,000	1914 S	4.50	5.00	10.00	32.50	100.00	400.00	
138,450	1915	16.00	22.50	40.00	62.50	115.00	575.00	675.00
1,170,400	1915 D	4.50	5.00	10.00	32.00	100.00	400.00	
1,604,000	1915 S	4.50	5.00	10.00	32.00	100.00	400.00	

HALF DOLLARS — WALKING LIBERTY TYPE

The mint marks are to the left of "half dollar" on the reverse.

Quantity	Year	Good	Very Good	Fine	Very Fine	Ext. Fine	Unc.
608,000	1916	$11.00	$20.00	$30.00	$40.00	$60.00	$215.00
1,014,400	1916 D on obv	6.00	9.00	16.00	30.00	50.00	200.00
508,000	1916 S on obv	20.00	30.00	50.00	85.00	125.00	375.00

Quantity	Year	Good	Very Good	Fine	Very Fine	Ext. Fine	Unc.
12,992,000	1917	$3.00	$3.75	$4.75	$8.00	$14.00	$65.00
765,400	1917 D on obv	6.00	9.00	20.00	42.50	75.00	225.00
1,940,000	1917 D on rev	3.75	4.50	10.00	25.00	60.00	250.00
952,000	1917 S on obv	7.00	9.50	22.50	60.00	125.00	600.00
5,554,000	1917 S on rev	3.00	3.50	5.50	12.50	30.00	225.00
6,634,000	1918	3.00	3.50	5.75	13.00	35.00	225.00
3,853,040	1918 D	3.00	4.00	7.50	24.00	55.00	250.00
10,282,000	1918 S	3.00	3.50	5.00	13.00	35.00	225.00
962,000	1919	5.50	7.00	15.00	45.00	110.00	750.00
1,165,000	1919 D	4.50	6.50	16.00	70.00	200.00	900.00
1,552,000	1919 S	3.50	5.50	14.00	60.00	175.00	1500.00
6,372,000	1920	3.00	3.75	5.00	13.00	35.00	200.00
1,551,000	1920 D	3.50	5.00	10.00	40.00	100.00	725.00
4,624,000	1920 S	3.00	3.75	8.00	25.00	70.00	650.00
246,000	1921	35.00	45.00	75.00	165.00	325.00	1500.00
208,000	1921 D	60.00	75.00	100.00	180.00	350.00	1800.00
548,000	1921 S	7.50	11.00	25.00	100.00	450.00	4000.00
2,178,000	1923 S	3.00	3.50	6.00	35.00	90.00	600.00
2,392,000	1927 S	3.00	3.50	5.00	12.00	45.00	375.00
1,940,000	1928 S		3.00	5.00	12.00	50.00	500.00
1,001,200	1929 D		4.50	6.50	10.00	40.00	200.00
1,902,000	1929 S		3.50	5.00	7.50	30.00	200.00
1,786,000	1933 S		3.25	4.25	6.00	20.00	220.00
6,964,000	1934		3.00	3.25	3.75	7.00	30.00
2,361,400	1934 D		3.25	4.00	4.75	15.00	72.50
3,652,000	1934 S		3.00	3.25	3.75	20.00	225.00
9,162,000	1935		3.00	3.25	3.75	6.00	26.00
3,003,800	1935 D		3.00	3.50	4.00	15.00	120.00
3,854,000	1935 S		3.00	3.50	3.75	22.00	195.00
12,617,901	1936		2.75	3.00	3.50	6.00	25.00
4,252,400	1936 D		2.75	3.00	5.00	8.00	60.00
3,884,000	1936 S		2.75	3.00	5.00	14.00	165.00
9,527,728	1937		2.75	3.00	3.50	5.50	26.00
1,760,001	1937 D		3.50	4.50	5.50	23.00	160.00
2,090,000	1937 S		2.75	3.25	4.50	16.00	110.00
4,118,152	1938		2.75	4.00	5.00	11.00	55.00
491,600	1938 D		26.00	28.50	32.50	65.00	350.00
6,820,808	1939		2.75	3.00	3.50	5.50	30.00
4,267,800	1939 D		2.75	3.00	3.75	6.00	30.00
2,552,000	1939 S		3.00	3.50	4.50	11.00	55.00
9,167,279	1940				3.00	5.00	25.00
4,550,000	1940 S				3.50	7.50	42.50
24,207,412	1941				3.00	4.50	20.00
11,248,400	1941 D				3.00	6.00	35.00
8,098,000	1941 S				5.00	12.50	80.00
47,839,120	1942				3.00	4.50	17.00
10,973,800	1942 D				4.50	7.50	27.50
12,708,000	1942 S				4.50	10.00	52.50
53,190,000	1943				3.00	4.50	17.50
11,346,000	1943 D				3.00	6.50	37.50
13,450,000	1943 S				3.00	6.00	26.50
28,206,000	1944				2.50	3.50	17.50
9,769,000	1944 D				3.00	4.50	22.50
8,904,000	1944 S				3.00	4.50	30.00
31,502,000	1945				2.50	3.50	17.50
9,966,800	1945 D				3.00	4.50	25.00
10,156,000	1945 S				3.00	4.50	26.50
12,118,000	1946				3.00	4.50	22.50
2,151,100	1946 D				3.00	4.50	26.50
3,724,000	1946 S				3.00	4.50	30.00
4,094,000	1947				3.00	4.50	25.00
3,900,000	1947 D				3.00	4.50	25.00

The mint marks are above the Liberty Bell on the reverse.

Quantity	Year	Very Fine	Ext. Fine	Unc.
3,006,814	1948	$3.00	$4.00	$12.50
4,028,600	1948 D	2.25	3.50	10.00
5,714,000	1949	4.00	6.00	35.00
4,120,600	1949 D	3.00	5.00	30.00
3,744,000	1949 S	4.50	6.50	42.00
7,793,509	1950	2.25	3.50	24.50
8,031,600	1950 D	1.75	3.00	16.00
16,859,602	1951	1.75	3.00	15.00
9,475,200	1951 D	1.75	3.50	24.00
13,696,000	1951 S	1.75	3.50	18.00
21,274,073	1952	1.25	2.50	12.00
25,395,600	1952 D	1.00	2.00	5.00
5,526,000	1952 S	1.50	3.50	23.00
2,796,920	1953	2.50	4.50	15.00
20,900,400	1953 D	1.00	2.00	5.00
4,148.000	1953 S	1.25	3.00	10.00
13,421,503	1954	1.00	2.00	4.00
25,445,580	1954 D	1.00	1.50	3.50
4,993,400	1954 S	1.25	2.00	5.00
2,876,381	1955	2.50	5.00	10.00

Quantity	Year	Ext. Fine	Unc.
4,213,081	1956	$1.75	$4.50
5,150,000	1957	1.50	4.25
19,966,850	1957 D	1.25	3.50
4,042,000	1958	1.50	4.00
23,962,412	1958 D	1.00	3.25
6,200,000	1959	1.50	4.00
13,053,750	1959 D	1.25	3.75
6,024,000	1960	1.50	4.00

Quantity	Year	Ext. Fine	Unc.
18,215,812	1960 D	$1.00	$3.25
11,318,244	1961	1.00	3.50
20,276,442	1961 D	1.00	3.25
12,932,019	1962	1.00	3.25
70,473,281	1962 D	1.00	3.25
	1963	1.00	3.25
	1963 D	1.00	3.25

HALF DOLLARS—KENNEDY TYPE

The mint marks are near the claw holding the laurel wreath on
the reverse.

Quantity	Year	Unc.	Quantity	Year	Unc.
273,304,004	1964	$2.50	3,267,667	1971 S (proof only)	
156,205,446	1964 D............	2.50	153,180,000	1972	$1.00
63,519,366	1965	1.50	141,890,000	1972 D............	1.00
106,723,349	1966	1.25	3,267,667	1972 S (proof only)	
295,046,978	1967	1.00	64,964,000	1973	1.00
246,951,930	1968 D............	1.00	83,171,400	1973 D............	1.00
3,041,509	1968 S (proof only)		2,769,624	1973 S (proof only)	
129,881,800	1969 D............	1.00	*	1974	1.00
2,934,631	1969 S (proof only)		*	1974 D............	1.00
2,150,000	1970 D............	17.50	2,617,350	1974 S (proof only)	
2,632,810	1970 S (proof only)		**	1976 Bicentennial reverse	
155,164,000	1971	1.00			
302,097,424	1971 D............	1.00	**	1976 D............	

* Mintage continued into 1975—struck simultaneously with Bicentennial
coins dated 1776–1976.
** Mintage of Bicentennial coins dated 1776–1976 began in March 1975.

Silver Dollars

DOLLARS — FLOWING HAIR TYPE

Quantity	Year	Good to Very Good	Fine	Very Fine
1,758	1794 very rare	$3750.00	$7000.00	$12,000.00
*	1795...	400.00	500.00	725.00

* This coin is included in quantity for 1795 draped bust type.

87

1795-1798   1798-1804

Quantity	Year	Good to Very Good	Fine	Very Fine
184,013	1795	$310.00	$500.00	$700.00
72,920	1796	285.00	450.00	575.00
7,776	1797 stars 10 and 6	310.00	500.00	650.00
	1797 stars 9 and 7	310.00	500.00	650.00
327,536	1798 small eagle, 15 stars	290.00	450.00	675.00
	1798 small eagle, 13 stars	290.00	450.00	675.00
327,536	1798 large eagle	260.00	375.00	500.00
423,515	1799 over 98, 15 stars	260.00	375.00	500.00
	1799 over 98, 13 stars	260.00	375.00	450.00
	1799 stars 7 and 6	260.00	375.00	450.00
	1799 stars 8 and 5	260.00	375.00	450.00
220,920	1800	260.00	375.00	450.00
54,454	1801	260.00	400.00	475.00
41,650	1802 over 1	260.00	400.00	475.00
	1802	260.00	375.00	450.00
66,064	1803	235.00	375.00	450.00
	1804 outstanding rarity			200,000.00

These beautiful pattern pieces from dies engraved by Christian Gobrecht were struck in 1836, 1838 and 1839 prior to the resumption of silver dollar coinage.

1836 pattern, proof condition	$3750.00
1838 pattern, proof condition	5000.00
1839 pattern, proof condition	5000.00

1840-1865   1866-1873

The mint marks are under the eagle on the reverse.

Quantity	Year	Good to Very Good	Fine	Very Fine	Ext. Fine	Unc.
61,005	1840	$85.00	$100.00	$115.00	$175.00	$750.00
173,000	1841	80.00	85.00	100.00	120.00	675.00
184,618	1842	80.00	85.00	100.00	120.00	625.00
165,100	1843	80.00	85.00	100.00	120.00	625.00
20,000	1844	85.00	95.00	120.00	175.00	750.00
24,500	1845	80.00	85.00	110.00	175.00	750.00
110,600	1846	80.00	85.00	100.00	120.00	625.00
59,000	1846 O	80.00	85.00	100.00	150.00	750.00
140,750	1847	80.00	85.00	100.00	120.00	625.00
15,000	1848	90.00	100.00	120.00	175.00	800.00
62,600	1849	80.00	85.00	110.00	150.00	750.00
7,500	1850	110.00	125.00	150.00	200.00	850.00
40,000	1850 O	85.00	100.00	110.00	150.00	850.00
1,300	1851	700.00	800.00	00.00	1750.00	2500.00
1,100	1852					3500.00
46,110	1853	85.00	100.00	125.00	200.00	800.00
33,140	1854	95.00	125.00	150.00	200.00	850.00
26,000	1855	90.00	125.00	175.00	300.00	1200.00
63,500	1856	90.00	110.00	125.00	200.00	750.00
94,000	1857	85.00	100.00	110.00	175.00	850.00
80	1858	Struck in proof only, 3250.00				
256,500	1859	80.00	85.00	90.00	110.00	650.00
360,000	1859 O	80.00	85.00	90.00	110.00	650.00
20,000	1859 S	90.00	100.00	120.00	175.00	1000.00
218,930	1860	80.00	85.00	90.00	110.00	650.00
515,000	1860 O	80.00	85.00	90.00	110.00	625.00
78,500	1861	80.00	85.00	95.00	125.00	625.00
12,090	1862	90.00	100.00	125.00	150.00	625.00
27,660	1863	85.00	95.00	110.00	140.00	625.00
31,170	1864	85.00	95.00	110.00	140.00	625.00
47,000	1865	80.00	90.00	100.00	130.00	625.00
49,625	1866 motto	80.00	90.00	100.00	130.00	625.00
60,325	1867	80.00	90.00	100.00	130.00	640.00
182,700	1868	80.00	90.00	95.00	110.00	640.00
424,300	1869	80.00	85.00	95.00	110.00	640.00
433,000	1870	80.00	85.00	95.00	110.00	640.00
?	1870 S extremely rare					
12,462	1870 CC	100.00	130.00	175.00	250.00	950.00
1,115,760	1871	80.00	85.00	95.00	110.00	640.00
1,376	1871 CC	450.00	650.00	1000.00	1500.00	4500.00
1,106,450	1872	80.00	85.00	95.00	110.00	640.00
9,000	1872 S	95.00	125.00	150.00	200.00	750.00
3,150	1872 CC	250.00	400.00	600.00	850.00	3200.00
293,600	1873	80.00	85.00	95.00	110.00	650.00
2,300	1873 CC	600.00	900.00	1200.00	2000.00	7500.00
700	1873 S extremely rare					

The mint mark is on the reverse under the eagle.

Quantity	Year	Fine	Very Fine	Ext. Fine	Unc.	Proof
10,509,550	1878 8 feathers......	$7.00	$8.50	$10.00	$22.00	$650.00
	1878 7 feathers......		7.50	8.50	14.00	1500.00
	1878 7 over 8					
	feathers	11 00	13.50	15.00	30.00	
9,774,000	1878 S		7.00	7.50	12.00	
2,212,000	1878 CC	9.50	10.50	14.00	30.00	
14,807,100	1879		7.00	7.50	13.00	550.00
2,887,000	1879 O	7.00	7.50	8.50	14.00	
9,110,000	1879 S		7.00	7.50	10.00	
756,000	1879 CC	25.00	37.00	90.00	575.00	
12,601,355	1880		7.00	7.50	12.00	550.00
5,305,000	1880 O	7.00	7.50	8.00	24.00	
8,900,000	1880 S		7.00	7.50	10.00	
591,000	1880 CC	28.00	37.50	47.50	67.50	
9,163,975	1881		7.00	7.50	13.00	550.00
5,708,000	1881 O	7.00	7.50	8.00	10.00	
12,760,000	1881 S	7.00	7.50	8.00	10.00	
296,000	1881 CC	55.00	60.00	65.00	75.00	
11,101,100	1882		7.00	7.50	11.00	550.00
6,090,000	1882 O	7.00	7.50	8.00	10.00	
9,250,000	1882 S		7.00	7.50	10.00	
1,133,000	1882 CC	14.50	16.50	20.00	30.00	
12,291,039	1883		7.00	7.50	11.00	550.00
8,725,000	1883 O		6.50	7.00	8.50	
6,250,000	1883 S	8.00	9.00	16.50	30.00	
1,204,000	1883 CC	14.50	16.50	20.00	24.00	
14,070,875	1884		7.00	7.50	11.00	550.00
9,730,000	1884 O		6.50	7.00	8.50	
3,200,000	1884 S	8.50	10.00	16.00	725.00	
1,136,000	1884 CC	25.00	26.50	28.50	37.50	
17,787,767	1885		6.50	7.00	9.00	550.00
9,185,000	1885 O		6.50	7.00	8.50	
1,497,000	1885 S	7.50	10.00	14.00	42.50	
228,000	1885 CC	37.50	45.00	50.00	75.00	
19,963,886	1886		6.50	7.00	9.00	550.00
10,710,000	1886 O	7.00	8.00	11.00	100.00	
750,000	1886 S	16.00	21.50	25.00	110.00	
20,290,710	1887		6.50	7.00	9.00	550.00
11,550,000	1887 O	7.00	7.50	8.00	18.00	
1,771,000	1887 S	8.50	9.50	12.50	40.00	
19,183,833	1888		6.50	7.00	9.00	550.00
12,150,000	1888 O	7.00	7.50	8.50	10.00	
657,000	1888 S	21.50	24.00	28.00	100.00	

Quantity	Year	Fine	Very Fine	Ext. Fine	Unc.	Proof
21,726,811	1889		$7.00	$7.50	$9.50	$550.00
11,875,000	1889 O	7.00	7.50	9.50	35.00	
700,000	1889 S	20.00	22.00	27.00	80.00	
350,000	1889 CC	85.00	110.00	325.00	3000.00	
16,802,590	1890		7.00	7.50	13.00	550.00
10,701,000	1890 O	7.00	7.50	8.00	24.00	
8,230,373	1890 S	7.00	7.50	8.50	26.00	
2,309,041	1890 CC	11.00	13.00	20.00	70.00	
8,694,206	1891	7.00	7.50	8.00	26.50	550.00
7,954,529	1891 O	7.00	7.50	8.00	32.50	
5,296,000	1891 S	7.00	8.00	8.50	27.00	
1,618,000	1891 CC	11.00	15.00	22.00	57.50	
1,037,245	1892	7.50	8.50	11.00	65.00	575.00
2,744,000	1892 O	7.50	8.50	11.00	62.50	
1,200,000	1892 S	9.00	17.50	80.00	12000.00	
1,352,000	1892 CC	21.00	30.00	52.50	180.00	
378,792	1893	16.50	20.00	30.00	185.00	650.00
300,000	1893 O	20.00	30.00	70.00	650.00	
100,000	1893 S	240.00	360.00	850.00	25000.00	
677,000	1893 CC	27.50	52.50	135.00	700.00	
110,972	1894	75.00	95.00	125.00	550.00	1200.00
1,723,000	1894 O	7.50	11.00	22.50	280.00	
1,260,000	1894 S	10.00	16.00	45.00	235.00	
12,880	1895 rare					8500.00
450,000	1895 O	22.00	35.00	80.00	1800.00	
400,000	1895 S	40.00	75.00	180.00	1750.00	
9,976,762	1896	7.00	7.50	8.00	12.00	550.00
4,900,000	1896 O	7.00	8.00	11.00	165.00	
5,000,000	1896 S	9.00	16.00	55.00	420.00	
2,822,731	1897	7.00	7.50	8.00	14.00	550.00
4,004,000	1897 O	7.00	7.50	11.00	135.00	
5,825,000	1897 S	7.00	8.00	9.00	13.00	
5,884,735	1898	7.00	7.50	8.00	13.00	550.00
4,440,000	1898 O	7.00	7.50	8.00	9.00	
4,102,000	1898 S	7.50	8.50	13.00	125.00	
330,846	1899	20.00	22.00	25.00	55.00	575.00
12,290,000	1899 O		7.00	7.50	9.00	
2,562,000	1899 S	7.00	11.00	20.00	200.00	
8,830,912	1900		7.00	7.50	9.50	550.00
12,590,000	1900 O		7.00	7.50	9.00	
3,540,000	1900 S	8.00	10.00	20.00	115.00	
6,962,813	1901	9.50	18.00	28.00	675.00	700.00
13,320,000	1901 O		7.00	7.50	12.00	
2,284,000	1901 S	9.00	11.00	18.00	125.00	
7,994,777	1902	7.00	7.50	8.00	27.00	550.00
8,636,000	1902 O		7.00	7.50	9.00	
1,530,000	1902 S	26.00	37.50	50.00	220.00	
4,652,755	1903	7.50	8.50	10.00	18.00	550.00
4,450,000	1903 O	32.50	37.50	40.00	55.00	
1,241,000	1903 S	9.00	16.00	60.00	1400.00	
2,788,650	1904	7.50	8.50	11.00	50.00	550.00
3,720,000	1904 O	7.00	7.50	8.00	9.00	
2,304,000	1904 S	8.50	11.00	35.00	475.00	
44,690,000	1921			7.00	7.50	
21,695,000	1921 S			7.50	14.00	
20,345,000	1921 D			7.50	15.00	

The mint marks are at the bottom to the left of the eagle's wing on the reverse.

Quantity	Year	Very Fine	Ext. Fine	Unc.
1,006,473	1921	$17.50	$25.00	$110.00
51,737,000	1922	4.50	6.50	8.00
15,063,000	1922 D	4.50	7.00	16.00
17,475,000	1922 S	4.50	7.00	15.00
30,800,000	1923	4.50	6.50	8.00
6,811,000	1923 D	4.50	7.00	16.00
19,020,000	1923 S	4.50	7.00	16.00
11,811,000	1924	4.50	7.00	9.00
1,728,000	1924 S	6.00	11.00	90.00
10,198,000	1925	4.50	7.00	9.00
1,610,000	1925 S	5.00	11.00	75.00
1,939,000	1926	5.00	9.50	20.00
2,348,700	1926 D	4.50	8.50	25.00
6,980,000	1926 S	4.50	8.50	24.00
848,000	1927	12.50	22.00	50.00
1,268,900	1927 D	7.50	12.50	85.00
866,000	1927 S	8.50	15.00	135.00
360,649	1928	65.00	100.00	175.00
1,632,000	1928 S	6.00	11.00	90.00
954,057	1934	12.50	20.00	50.00
1,569,000	1934 D	7.50	13.00	70.00
1,011,000	1934 S	25.00	50.00	750.00
1,576,000	1935	7.50	15.00	45.00
1,964,000	1935 S	8.50	18.00	115.00

Quantity	Year	Unc.
47,799,000	1971..................	$1.85
68,587,424	1971 D	1.75
6,668,526	1971 S	4.50
75,890,000	1972..................	1.85
95,548,511	1972 D	1.75
2,193,056	1972 S	4.50
2,000,056	1973..................	7.00
2,000,000	1973 D	7.00
1,883,140	1973 S	6.50
27,366,000	1974..................	1.75
35,466,000	1974 D	1.75
1,900,000	1974 S	4.50
**	1976 Bicentennial reverse	
**	1976 D	

** Mintage of Bicentennial coins dated 1776 – 1976 began in February 1975.

Trade Dollars

These silver coins were issued from 1873 to 1885 for use in the Orient. From 1879 to 1885 Trade Dollars were issued only as proofs, apparently for collectors. It is said that Trade Dollars are still circulating in the Orient—some of them mutilated by "chopmarks" made to check their content.

The mint marks are under the eagle on the reverse.

Quantity	Year	Good to Very Good	Fine	Very Fine	Ext. Fine	Unc.	Proof
397,500	1873	$50.00	$55.00	$65.00	$90.00	$400.00	$1500.00
703,000	1873 S	50.00	55.00	70.00	90.00	375.00	
124,500	1873 CC	55.00	65.00	90.00	150.00	600.00	
987,800	1874	50.00	55.00	65.00	90.00	350.00	1450.00
2,549,000	1874 S	50.00	55.00	65.00	90.00	350.00	
1,373,200	1874 CC	55.00	60.00	75.00	100.00	500.00	
218,900	1875	55.00	65.00	85.00	125.00	500.00	1500.00
4,487,000	1875 S	50.00	55.00	65.00	85.00	350.00	
1,573,700	1875 CC	55.00	65.00	75.00	100.00	550.00	
456,150	1876	50.00	55.00	65.00	85.00	375.00	1450.00
5,227,000	1876 S	50.00	55.00	65.00	85.00	350.00	
509,000	1876 CC	55.00	65.00	85.00	120.00	500.00	
3,039,710	1877	50.00	55.00	65.00	85.00	350.00	1450.00
9,519,000	1877 S	50.00	55.00	65.00	85.00	350.00	
534,000	1877 CC	60.00	90.00	120.00	150.00	750.00	
900	1878 Proofs only						1600.00
4,162,000	1878 S	50.00	55.00	65.00	85.00	350.00	
97,000	1878 CC	110.00	200.00	275.00	450.00	2500.00	
1,541	1879 Proofs only						1600.00
1,987	1880 Proofs only						1600.00
960	1881 Proofs only						1600.00
1,097	1882 Proofs only						1600.00
979	1883 Proofs only						1600.00
10	1884 Proofs only					Extremely rare	
5	1885 Proofs only					Extremely rare	

GOLD COINS

There are a number of reasons why gold coins are scarce and have substantial values. Gold is intrinsically much more valuable than silver, and there have been times when it was desirable to melt down gold coins for what the metal would bring.

Remember, also, that up to the time gold was discovered in California in 1848, the metal was scarce in the United States. Consequently the early issues of gold coins were small and the coins correspondingly scarce. Then, too, gold coins never circulated to more than a very limited extent; collectors did not come across these coins in ordinary usage.

Still another reason for the present-day scarcity of gold coins is the Presidential Order of 1933 which removed gold coins from circulation. (The order, by the way, made a careful distinction in favor of coin collectors by allowing them to continue acquiring gold coins as part of their hobby.)

Gold coins were struck in the following denominations:

Gold Dollars	1849-1889
Quarter Eagles ($2.50)	1796-1929
Three-Dollar Gold Pieces	1854-1889
Half Eagles ($5)	1795-1929
Eagles ($10)	1795-1933
Double Eagles ($20)	1849-1933

Gold Dollars

These coins were first issued when gold became plentiful after the California Gold Rush. They are very small, weighing only 25.8 grains. (A silver dollar weighs over 400 grains.)

Liberty Head Type

The mint mark is below the wreath on the reverse.

Liberty Head Type

Quantity	Year	Fine	Very Fine	Unc.
658,567	1849 open wreath —small head and stars	$120.00	$150.00	$300.00
	1849 open wreath —large head and stars	120.00	140.00	300.00
	1849 closed wreath	120.00	140.00	300.00
?	1849 C open wreath (extremely rare)			
11,634	1849 C closed wreath	150.00	350.00	1600.00
21,588	1849 D open wreath	200.00	300.00	1200.00
215,000	1849 O open wreath	120.00	200.00	500.00
481,953	1850	120.00	150.00	300.00
6,966	1850 C	250.00	400.00	1350.00
8,382	1850 D	225.00	275.00	1200.00
14,000	1850 O	120.00	200.00	550.00
3,317,671	1851	120.00	150.00	285.00
41,267	1851 C	200.00	300.00	1000.00
9,882	1851 D	225.00	350.00	1250.00
290,000	1851 O	120.00	150.00	400.00
2,045,351	1852	120.00	150.00	285.00
9,434	1852 C	225.00	350.00	1200.00
6,360	1852 D	225.00	350.00	1250.00
140,000	1852 O	120.00	150.00	500.00
4,076,051	1853	120.00	150.00	285.00
11,515	1853 C	200.00	300.00	1200.00
6,583	1853 D	225.00	350.00	1250.00
290,000	1853 O	120.00	150.00	425.00
1,639,445*	1854	120.00	150.00	285.00
2,935	1854 D	350.00	600.00	3000.00
14,632	1854 S	150.00	250.00	1200.00

* includes Indian-Headdress Dollars of 1854

Indian-Headdress Type

Quantity	Year	Fine	Very Fine	Unc.
*	1854	250.00	350.00	2800.00
758,269	1855	250.00	350.00	2800.00
9,803	1855 C	400.00	650.00	3500.00
1,811	1855 D	1750.00	2700.00	6000.00
55,000	1855 O	400.00	500.00	3250.00
24,600	1856 S	250.00	400.00	3000.00

Larger Indian-Headdress Type

Quantity	Year	Fine	Very Fine	Unc.
1,762,936	1856	120.00	140.00	350.00
1,460	1856 D	1750.00	3000.00	7500.00
774,789	1857	120.00	140.00	300.00
13,280	1857 C	225.00	400.00	1000.00
3,533	1857 D	400.00	600.00	2500.00
10,000	1857 S	150.00	300.00	550.00

Quantity	Year	Fine	Very Fine	Unc.
	Larger Indian-Headdress Type			
117,995	1858	$120.00	$140.00	$300.00
3,477	1858 D	500.00	800.00	2500.00
10,000	1858 S	120.00	175.00	400.00
168,244	1859	120.00	140.00	300.00
5,235	1859 C	200.00	350.00	1100.00
4,952	1859 D	250.00	400.00	1750.00
15,000	1859 S	120.00	175.00	500.00
36,668	1860	120.00	140.00	285.00
1,556	1860 D	2000.00	3500.00	8500.00
13,000	1860 S	120.00	200.00	750.00
527,499	1861	120.00	140.00	285.00
?	1861 D	3500.00	5500.00	17,500.00
1,326,865	1862	120.00	140.00	275.00
6,250	1863	200.00	350.00	1150.00
5,950	1864	175.00	300.00	950.00
3,725	1865	200.00	300.00	1100.00
7,180	1866	150.00	250.00	700.00
5,250	1867	150.00	250.00	750.00
10,525	1868	125.00	200.00	725.00
5,925	1869	135.00	240.00	650.00
6,335	1870	130.00	225.00	650.00
3,000	1870 S	350.00	500.00	3000.00
3,930	1871	175.00	300.00	800.00
3,530	1872	175.00	300.00	800.00
125,125	1873	150.00	250.00	400.00
198,820	1874	120.00	140.00	275.00
420	1875	2000.00	3500.00	7500.00
3,425	1876	125.00	225.00	750.00
3,920	1877	175.00	300.00	800.00
3,020	1878	150.00	250.00	725.00
3,030	1879	150.00	250.00	700.00
1,636	1880	125.00	200.00	700.00
7,660	1881	125.00	175.00	500.00
5,040	1882	120.00	150.00	450.00
10,840	1883	120.00	140.00	450.00
6,206	1884	120.00	140.00	450.00
12,205	1885	120.00	135.00	450.00
6,016	1886	120.00	145.00	450.00
8,543	1887	120.00	140.00	450.00
16,080	1888	120.00	135.00	450.00
30,729	1889	120.00	135.00	425.00

Quarter Eagles ($2.50)

The handsome Indian Head Type in the quarter eagle and half eagle series is unique in United States coinage in that the design and legends are incused. This means they are sunk below the surface of the coin instead of being in relief (raised above the surface of the coin).

QUARTER EAGLES ($2.50 GOLD PIECES)
Liberty Cap Type

Quantity	Year	Fine	Very Fine	Unc.
897	1796 no stars	$5000.00	$7000.00	$20,000.00
66	1796 with stars	4500.00	6000.00	15,000.00
1,756	1797	3000.00	4500.00	12,000.00
614	1798	2000.00	3000.00	7000.00
2,612	1802 over 1	1000.00	1500.00	5500.00
3,327	1804	2000.00	3000.00	9000.00
1,781	1805	1100.00	1800.00	5500.00
1,616 {	1806 over 4	1250.00	2000.00	6000.00
	1806 over 5	2000.00	2500.00	6500.00
6,812	1807	1000.00	1500.00	4500.00

Liberty Head With Motto Over Eagle

2,710	1808	4500.00	7000.00	17,500.00
6,448	1821 reduced size	1000.00	1500.00	5500.00
2,600	1824 over 21	1000.00	1500.00	6000.00
4,434	1825	1000.00	1500.00	5750.00
760	1826 over 25	1250.00	2000.00	10,000.00
2,800	1827	1000.00	1500.00	5500.00
3,403	1829	1000.00	1500.00	5250.00
4,540	1830	1000.00	1500.00	5000.00
4,520	1831	1000.00	1500.00	5000.00
4,400	1832	1000.00	1500.00	5000.00
4,160	1833	1000.00	1500.00	5000.00
4,000	1834	2000.00	3000.00	15,000.00

Ribbon Type Without Motto

The mint mark—only on 1838 and 1839—is above the date on the obverse.

112,324	1834	125.00	200.00	2250.00
131,402	1835	125.00	200.00	2250.00
547,986	1836	125.00	200.00	2250.00
45,080	1837	135.00	200.00	2500.00
47,030	1838	135.00	200.00	2500.00
7,908	1838 C	250.00	450.00	3500.00
27,021	1839	135.00	200.00	2750.00
18,173	1839 C	200.00	300.00	3000.00
13,674	1839 D	200.00	300.00	3000.00
17,781	1839 O	200.00	250.00	2750.00

The mint mark is below the eagle on the reverse.

Quantity	Year	Fine	Very Fine	Unc.
18,859	1840	$100.00	$150.00	$500.00
12,838	1840 C	200.00	350.00	1250.00
3,532	1840 D	250.00	400.00	1500.00
26,200	1840 O	100.00	150.00	500.00
?	1841 (an outstanding rarity; Proof $26,000.00)			
10,297	1841 C	200.00	325.00	1150.00
4,164	1841 D	225.00	400.00	1250.00
2,823	1842	250.00	400.00	1250.00
6,737	1842 C	225.00	350.00	1250.00
4,643	1842 D	225.00	400.00	1500.00
19,800	1842 O	115.00	175.00	450.00
100,546	1843	95.00	125.00	350.00
26,096	1843 C	250.00	400.00	1500.00
36,209	1843 D	200.00	325.00	1250.00
368,002	1843 O	100.00	150.00	500.00
6,784	1844	200.00	400.00	1000.00
11,622	1844 C	200.00	300.00	1000.00
17,732	1844 D	200.00	300.00	1000.00
91,051	1845	85.00	125.00	275.00
19,460	1845 D	200.00	300.00	1000.00
4,000	1845 O	300.00	600.00	2500.00
21,598	1846	80.00	125.00	300.00
4,808	1846 C	250.00	500.00	1800.00
19,303	1846 D	200.00	350.00	1750.00
66,000	1846 O	85.00	125.00	350.00
29,814	1847	85.00	125.00	300.00
23,226	1847 C	200.00	325.00	1600.00
15,784	1847 D	200.00	325.00	1850.00
124,000	1847 O	85.00	125.00	375.00
8,886 {	1848	350.00	550.00	1500.00
	1848 CAL over eagle (rare)	2500.00	4000.00	12,500.00
16,788	1848 C	200.00	300.00	1750.00
13,771	1848 D	200.00	300.00	2000.00
23,294	1849	85.00	125.00	300.00
10,220	1849 C	200.00	350.00	1500.00
10,945	1849 D	200.00	400.00	1650.00
252,923	1850	85.00	125.00	250.00
9,148	1850 C	200.00	300.00	1100.00
12,148	1850 D	200.00	300.00	1000.00
84,000	1850 O	85.00	125.00	325.00
1,372,648	1851	75.00	100.00	250.00
14,923	1851 C	200.00	300.00	1100.00
11,264	1851 D	200.00	300.00	1100.00
148,000	1851 O	85.00	125.00	300.00
1,159,681	1852	85.00	100.00	250.00
9,772	1852 C	200.00	300.00	1250.00
4,078	1852 D	250.00	450.00	1650.00
140,000	1852 O	85.00	125.00	400.00
1,404,668	1853	85.00	100.00	250.00
3,178	1853 D	350.00	500.00	2750.00

Quantity	Year	Fine	Very Fine	Unc.
	Coronet Type Without Motto			
596,258	1854	$75.00	$100.00	$250.00
7,295	1854 C	200.00	300.00	1250.00
1,760	1854 D	1200.00	2000.00	6000.00
153,000	1854 O	75.00	125.00	325.00
246	1854 S	10,000.00	20,000.00	50,000.00
235,480	1855	75.00	125.00	250.00
3,677	1855 C	500.00	800.00	3000.00
1,123	1855 D	1000.00	2000.00	6000.00
384,240	1856	75.00	125.00	250.00
7,913	1856 C	225.00	350.00	1250.00
874	1856 D	2000.00	4000.00	12,000.00
21,100	1856 O	85.00	125.00	400.00
71,120	1856 S	85.00	150.00	650.00
214,130	1857	75.00	100.00	250.00
2,364	1857 D	375.00	550.00	2400.00
34,000	1857 O	75.00	125.00	350.00
68,000	1857 S	85.00	125.00	650.00
47,377	1858	75.00	125.00	750.00
9,056	1858 C	200.00	300.00	1200.00
39,444	1859	75.00	125.00	275.00
2,244	1859 D	300.00	550.00	2000.00
15,200	1859 S	100.00	150.00	250.00
22,675	1860	75.00	125.00	250.00
7,469	1860 C	200.00	350.00	1200.00
35,600	1860 S	85.00	125.00	450.00
1,272,518	1861	75.00	95.00	225.00
24,000	1861 S	75.00	125.00	500.00
112,353	1862	75.00	95.00	250.00
8,000	1862 S	125.00	200.00	1000.00
30	1863 very rare (only proofs were struck 50,000.00)			
10,800	1863 S	100.00	150.00	600.00
2,874	1864	300.00	500.00	1800.00
1,545	1865	325.00	500.00	1800.00
23,376	1865 S	90.00	135.00	450.00
3,110	1866	175.00	275.00	850.00
38,960	1866 S	85.00	125.00	450.00
3,250	1867	200.00	300.00	950.00
28,000	1867 S	85.00	125.00	400.00
3,625	1868	175.00	275.00	800.00
34,000	1868 S	85.00	125.00	375.00
4,345	1869	125.00	175.00	500.00
29,500	1869 S	85.00	125.00	375.00
4,555	1870	125.00	175.00	550.00
16,000	1870 S	85.00	125.00	400.00
5,350	1871	125.00	175.00	550.00
22,000	1871 S	85.00	125.00	375.00
3,030	1872	175.00	250.00	650.00
178,025	1873	75.00	85.00	185.00
27,000	1873 S	85.00	125.00	250.00
3,940	1874	150.00	200.00	600.00
420	1875	1500.00	2000.00	6000.00
11,600	1875 S	100.00	150.00	450.00
4,221	1876	125.00	200.00	600.00
5,000	1876 S	95.00	125.00	350.00
1,652	1877	325.00	450.00	1200.00
35,400	1877 S	80.00	95.00	200.00
286,260	1878	75.00	85.00	165.00
178,000	1878 S	75.00	85.00	165.00
88,900	1879	75.00	85.00	175.00
43,500	1879 S	75.00	85.00	185.00
2,996	1880	140.00	185.00	550.00
680	1881	325.00	500.00	1500.00
4,040	1882	125.00	165.00	475.00

QUARTER EAGLES (continued)

Quantity	Year	Fine	Very Fine	Unc.
		Coronet Type Without Motto		
1,960	1883	$150.00	$200.00	$525.00
1,993	1884	150.00	200.00	550.00
887	1885	300.00	500.00	1850.00
4,088	1886	125.00	150.00	475.00
6,282	1887	100.00	150.00	350.00
16,098	1888	75.00	95.00	225.00
17,648	1889	75.00	95.00	225.00
8,813	1890	85.00	110.00	275.00
11,040	1891	75.00	95.00	225.00
2,545	1892	125.00	150.00	450.00
30,106	1893	75.00	95.00	175.00
4,122	1894	85.00	120.00	350.00
6,119	1895	85.00	120.00	300.00
19,202	1896	75.00	90.00	175.00
29,904	1897	75.00	90.00	175.00
24,165	1898	75.00	90.00	175.00
27,350	1899	75.00	90.00	175.00
67,205	1900	75.00	90.00	165.00
91,323	1901	75.00	90.00	165.00
133,733	1902	75.00	90.00	165.00
201,257	1903	75.00	90.00	165.00
160,960	1904	75.00	90.00	165.00
217,944	1905	75.00	90.00	165.00
176,490	1906	75.00	90.00	165.00
336,448	1907	75.00	90.00	165.00

Indian Head Incuse Type

The mint mark is to the left of the eagle's claw on the reverse.

Quantity	Year	Very Fine	Ext. Fine	Unc.
565,057	1908	$80.00	$100.00	$200.00
441,899	1909	80.00	100.00	155.00
492,682	1910	80.00	100.00	155.00
704,191	1911	80.00	100.00	155.00
55,680	1911 D	425.00	650.00	1500.00
616,197	1912	80.00	100.00	155.00
722,165	1913	80.00	100.00	155.00
240,117	1914	80.00	100.00	250.00
448,000	1914 D	80.00	100.00	155.00
606,100	1915	80.00	100.00	150.00
578,000	1925 D	80.00	100.00	150.00
446,000	1926	80.00	100.00	150.00
388,000	1927	80.00	100.00	150.00
416,000	1928	80.00	100.00	150.00
532,000	1929	80.00	100.00	150.00

Three Dollar Gold Pieces

Like the three-cent pieces, these coins were intended for buying three-cent stamps. However, the public remained indifferent to both types of coins. When the postal rate was changed, the coinage of these gold pieces came to an end.

THREE-DOLLAR GOLD PIECES

The mint mark is below the wreath on the reverse.

Quantity	Year	Fine	Very Fine	Unc.
138,618	1854	$300.00	$450.00	$2250.00
1,120	1854 D	2000.00	3000.00	6000.00
24,000	1854 O	300.00	475.00	2750.00
50,555	1855	300.00	450.00	2750.00
6,600	1855 S	350.00	500.00	3000.00
26,010	1856	300.00	450.00	2000.00
34,500	1856 S small S	300.00	475.00	2250.00
20,891	1857	300.00	450.00	2000.00
14,000	1857 S	320.00	475.00	2250.00
2,133	1858	350.00	500.00	2500.00
15,638	1859	300.00	450.00	2250.00
7,155	1860	350.00	500.00	2750.00
7,000	1860 S	325.00	475.00	3500.00
6,072	1861	350.00	500.00	2750.00
5,785	1862	325.00	475.00	2500.00
5,039	1863	400.00	600.00	3200.00
2,680	1864	400.00	600.00	3250.00
1,165	1865	500.00	700.00	3500.00
4,030	1866	325.00	425.00	2500.00
2,650	1867	375.00	550.00	3250.00
4,875	1868	325.00	475.00	2500.00
2,525	1869	375.00	550.00	3000.00
3,535	1870	325.00	450.00	2500.00
2	1870 S unique			
1,330	1871	350.00	550.00	2750.00
2,030	1872	325.00	500.00	2500.00
25	1873 (only proofs were struck)	10,000.00		
41,820	1874	300.00	450.00	1800.00
20	1875 (only proofs were struck)	150,000.00		
45	1876 (only proofs were struck)	21,000.00		
1,488	1877	400.00	600.00	4000.00
82,234	1878	300.00	450.00	1750.00
3,030	1879	350.00	500.00	2750.00
1,036	1880	350.00	675.00	3000.00
550	1881	900.00	1200.00	4000.00
1,540	1882	350.00	500.00	2500.00
940	1883	350.00	750.00	3250.00
1,106	1884	350.00	500.00	3000.00
910	1885	350.00	525.00	3250.00
1,142	1886	350.00	500.00	2750.00
6,160	1887	325.00	475.00	2250.00
5,291	1888	325.00	475.00	2100.00
2,429	1889	325.00	600.00	2250.00

Four-Dollar Gold Pieces

These coins are sometimes called "Stellas" because of the star on the obverse. Though struck as patterns in 1879 and 1880, they were never issued as regular coins. The decision not to use them was a sensible one, as three-dollar and five-dollar gold pieces were already in existence.

The "Stellas" were struck in very small quantities and are therefore among the highly prized rarities of American coinage.

FOUR-DOLLAR ("STELLA") GOLD PIECE PATTERNS
(only proofs were struck)

Quantity	Year	Proof
415	1879 flowing hair	$25,000.00
10	1879 coiled hair	50,000.00
15	1880 flowing hair	35,000.00
10	1880 coiled hair	60,000.00

Half Eagles ($5)

It is curious that up to 1807 these coins carried no indication of their value.

HALF EAGLES ($5 GOLD PIECES)
Bust Type Facing Right

1795-1798   1795-1807

HALF EAGLES (continued)

Quantity	Year	Fine	Very Fine	Unc.
	Bust Type Facing Right			
8,707 {	1795 small eagle	$2000.00	$3500.00	$10,000.00
	1795 large eagle	2500.00	3750.00	12,500.00
3,399	1796 over 95 small eagle	2000.00	3500.00	9000.00
6,406 {	1797 over 95 large eagle	2500.00	3500.00	8500.00
	1797 15 stars small eagle	2500.00	6000.00	12,000.00
	1797 16 stars small eagle	2000.00	3500.00	10,000.00
24,867 {	1798 small eagle	2500.00	5000.00	8500.00
	1798 large eagle	700.00	1250.00	4500.00
7,451	1799	650.00	1000.00	3750.00
11,622	1800	600.00	850.00	3000.00
53,176	1802 over 1	600.00	850.00	3000.00
33,506	1803 over 2	600.00	850.00	1000.00
30,475	1804	650.00	850.00	3600.00
33,183	1805	650.00	1000.00	3500.00
64,093	1806	650.00	900.00	3500.00
33,496	1807	600.00	900.00	3250.00

Bust Type Facing Left

1807-1812   1813-1834

Quantity	Year	Fine	Very Fine	Unc.
50,597	1807	575.00	800.00	2750.00
55,578 {	1808 over 7	650.00	950.00	3000.00
	1808	575.00	800.00	2750.00
33,875 {	1809 over 8	575.00	800.00	2750.00
	1809	575.00	800.00	2750.00
100,287	1810	650.00	900.00	3000.00
99,581	1811	625.00	900.00	2850.00
58,087	1812	550.00	750.00	2500.00
95,428	1813 larger head	650.00	900.00	3000.00
15,454	1814	1000.00	2000.00	5500.00
635	1815			10,000.00
45,588	1818	1000.00	2250.00	6000.00
51,723	1819	5500.00	7000.00	12,500.00
263,806	1820	750.00	1250.00	3500.00
34,641	1821	2500.00	4000.00	10,000.00
17,796	1822 an outstanding rarity			35,000.00
14,485	1823	2000.00	3000.00	6000.00
17,340	1824	3000.00	5000.00	12,500.00
29,060 {	1825 over 21	2500.00	4000.00	10,000.00
	1825 over 24	2750.00	5000.00	10,000.00
18,069	1826 rare	1500.00	2750.00	6000.00
24,913	1827	6000.00	8000.00	12,000.00
28,029 {	1828 over 27	1500.00	2750.00	7500.00
	1828	2500.00	3500.00	10,000.00

HALF EAGLES (continued)

Quantity	Year	Fine	Very Fine	Unc.

Bust Type Facing Left

Quantity	Year	Fine	Very Fine	Unc.
57,442	1829			$23,500.00
126,351	1830	$1250.00	$2000.00	6500.00
140,594	1831	1250.00	2000.00	6750.00
157,487	1832 curled 2, 12 stars	5000.00	7000.00	20,000.00
	1832 square-based 2, 13 stars	2500.00	4000.00	15,000.00
193,630	1833	1200.00	1800.00	5000.00
50,141	1834	1250.00	2000.00	7000.00

Ribbon Type Without Motto

The mint mark—only on 1838—is above the date on the obverse.

Quantity	Year	Fine	Very Fine	Unc.
682,028	1834	175.00	250.00	2000.00
371,534	1835	160.00	225.00	2000.00
553,147	1836	160.00	225.00	2000.00
207,121	1837	175.00	240.00	2200.00
286,588	1838	175.00	240.00	2200.00
12,913	1838 C	525.00	875.00	3500.00
20,583	1838 D	525.00	775.00	3500.00

Coronet Type

1839-1865   1866- 1908

The mint mark is below the eagle on the reverse.

Quantity	Year	Fine	Very Fine	Unc.
118,143	1839	125.00	175.00	750.00
23,467	1839 C	250.00	400.00	1500.00
18,939	1839 D	250.00	400.00	1500.00
137,382	1840	100.00	125.00	500.00
19,028	1840 C	225.00	350.00	1300.00
22,896	1840 D	225.00	350.00	1375.00
30,400	1840 O	125.00	175.00	750.00
15,833	1841	125.00	200.00	650.00
21,511	1841 C	225.00	350.00	1500.00
30,495	1841 D	225.00	350.00	1250.00
8,350	1841 O (2 known)			
27,578	1842	100.00	150.00	750.00
27,480	1842 C	225.00	350.00	1250.00
59,608	1842 D	225.00	350.00	1250.00
16,400	1842 O	110.00	175.00	750.00

Quantity	Year	Fine	Very Fine	Unc.
	Coronet Type			
611,205	1843	$90.00	$110.00	$400.00
44,353	1843 C	200.00	300.00	1150.00
98,452	1843 D	200.00	300.00	1100.00
101,075	1843 O	125.00	185.00	650.00
340,330	1844	90.00	110.00	1100.00
23,631	1844 C	200.00	300.00	1300.00
88,982	1844 D	200.00	400.00	1500.00
364,600	1844 O	125.00	250.00	600.00
417,099	1845	90.00	110.00	400.00
90,629	1845 D	200.00	350.00	1400.00
41,000	1845 O	125.00	275.00	1000.00
395,942	1846	90.00	110.00	400.00
12,995	1846 C	225.00	400.00	1250.00
80,294	1846 D	200.00	300.00	1200.00
58,000	1846 O	125.00	200.00	700.00
915,981	1847	90.00	110.00	400.00
84,151	1847 C	225.00	325.00	1000.00
64,405	1847 D	200.00	300.00	1150.00
12,000	1847 O	150.00	325.00	1400.00
260,775	1848	90.00	110.00	450.00
64,472	1848 C	225.00	325.00	1200.00
47,465	1848 D	225.00	325.00	1200.00
133,070	1849	90.00	110.00	425.00
64,823	1849 C	225.00	325.00	1250.00
39,036	1849 D	225.00	325.00	1200.00
64,491	1850	100.00	125.00	450.00
63,591	1850 C	200.00	300.00	1150.00
43,950	1850 D	200.00	300.00	1200.00
377,505	1851	90.00	110.00	350.00
49,176	1851 C	225.00	325.00	1250.00
62,710	1851 D	200.00	300.00	1200.00
41,000	1851 O	150.00	250.00	900.00
573,901	1852	90.00	110.00	350.00
72,574	1852 C	225.00	325.00	1350.00
91,452	1852 D	225.00	325.00	1200.00
305,770	1853	90.00	110.00	370.00
65,571	1853 C	225.00	325.00	1250.00
89,678	1853 D	200.00	300.00	1350.00
160,675	1854	90.00	110.00	400.00
39,291	1854 C	200.00	300.00	1250.00
56,413	1854 D	200.00	300.00	1150.00
46,000	1854 O	125.00	250.00	700.00
268	1854 S ext. rare			
117,098	1855	90.00	110.00	400.00
39,788	1855 C	200.00	300.00	1100.00
22,432	1855 D	200.00	300.00	1200.00
11,100	1855 O	150.00	275.00	1000.00
61,000	1855 S	90.00	125.00	650.00
197,990	1856	90.00	110.00	400.00
28,457	1856 C	250.00	400.00	1150.00
19,786	1856 D	225.00	325.00	1250.00
10,000	1856 O	200.00	400.00	1500.00
105,100	1856 S	100.00	150.00	650.00
98,188	1857	90.00	110.00	400.00
31,360	1857 C	225.00	425.00	1300.00
17,046	1857 D	225.00	450.00	1500.00
13,000	1857 O	150.00	450.00	1000.00
87,000	1857 S	90.00	115.00	650.00
15,136	1858	135.00	200.00	700.00
38,856	1858 C	200.00	400.00	1250.00
15,362	1858 D	225.00	325.00	1500.00
18,600	1858 S	175.00	275.00	850.00
16,814	1859	125.00	175.00	600.00

Quantity	Year	Fine	Very Fine	Unc.
		Coronet Type		
31,847	1859 C	$200.00	$300.00	$1200.00
10,366	1859 D	250.00	375.00	1350.00
13,220	1859 S	175.00	275.00	750.00
19,825	1860	120.00	175.00	600.00
14,813	1860 C	225.00	400.00	1500.00
14,635	1860 D	225.00	400.00	1500.00
21,200	1860 S	125.00	175.00	700.00
639,950	1861	85.00	100.00	300.00
6,879	1861 C	850.00	1200.00	4000.00
1,597	1861 D	3000.00	4250.00	11,000.00
18,000	1861 S	150.00	225.00	850.00
4,465	1862	225.00	325.00	1000.00
9,500	1862 S	150.00	250.00	900.00
2,472	1863	400.00	600.00	2000.00
17,000	1863 S	200.00	300.00	1000.00
4,220	1864	275.00	375.00	1800.00
3,888	1864 S	1000.00	1750.00	5000.00
1,295	1865	400.00	600.00	2000.00
27,612	1865 S	125.00	200.00	550.00
43,920*	1866 S no motto	175.00	300.00	875.00
		Coronet Type With Motto		

The mint mark is below the eagle on the reverse.

Quantity	Year	Fine	Very Fine	Unc.
6,720	1866	225.00	375.00	1000.00
*	1866 S	150.00	300.00	1250.00
6,920	1867	150.00	300.00	1000.00
29,000	1867 S	125.00	225.00	650.00
5,725	1868	175.00	300.00	750.00
52,000	1868 S	125.00	175.00	650.00
1,785	1869	400.00	600.00	1200.00
31,000	1869 S	150.00	200.00	600.00
4,035	1870	200.00	350.00	850.00
7,675	1870 CC	1200.00	2000.00	5000.00
17,000	1870 S	125.00	175.00	700.00
3,230	1871	250.00	400.00	1000.00
20,770	1871 CC	400.00	550.00	1000.00
25,000	1871 S	125.00	200.00	600.00
1,690	1872	400.00	500.00	1250.00
16,980	1872 CC	350.00	600.00	1000.00
36,400	1872 S	125.00	175.00	550.00
112,505	1873	85.00	125.00	185.00
7,416	1873 CC	400.00	750.00	2000.00
31,000	1873 S	100.00	175.00	600.00
3,508	1874	250.00	500.00	1150.00
21,198	1874 CC	250.00	400.00	1500.00
16,000	1874 S	125.00	250.00	500.00
220	1875 rare	2000.00	3500.00	10,000.00
11,828	1875 CC	350.00	600.00	1200.00
9,000	1875 S	150.00	250.00	1000.00
1,477	1876	400.00	650.00	2250.00
6,887	1876 CC	400.00	600.00	1850.00
4,000	1876 S	300.00	600.00	1750.00
1,152	1877	400.00	600.00	2000.00
8,680	1877 CC	300.00	500.00	1850.00
26,700	1877 S	100.00	135.00	350.00
131,740	1878	75.00	90.00	135.00
9,054	1878 CC	750.00	2000.00	5000.00
144,700	1878 S	75.00	90.00	135.00
301,950	1879	75.00	90.00	135.00
17,281	1879 CC	175.00	275.00	750.00
426,200	1879 S	75.00	90.00	135.00

* Includes 1866 S coins with motto.

Quantity	Year	Fine	Very Fine	Unc.
	Coronet Type With Motto			
3,166,436	1880	$75.00	$85.00	$125.00
51,017	1880 CC	125.00	175.00	550.00
1,348,900	1880 S	75.00	85.00	125.00
5,708,800	1881	75.00	85.00	125.00
13,886	1881 CC	150.00	200.00	550.00
969,000	1881 S	75.00	85.00	125.00
2,514,560	1882	75.00	85.00	125.00
82,817	1882 CC	100.00	150.00	350.00
969,000	1882 S	75.00	85.00	125.00
233,440	1883	75.00	90.00	135.00
12,598	1883 CC	135.00	200.00	400.00
83,200	1883 S	75.00	90.00	150.00
191,048	1884	75.00	90.00	135.00
16,402	1884 CC	100.00	150.00	450.00
177,000	1884 S	75.00	90.00	135.00
601,506	1885	75.00	85.00	125.00
1,211,500	1885 S	75.00	85.00	125.00
388,432	1886	75.00	90.00	135.00
3,268,000	1886 S	75.00	85.00	125.00
87	1887 rare (only proofs were struck)		20,000.00	
1,912,000	1887 S	75.00	90.00	125.00
18,296	1888	90.00	110.00	200.00
293,900	1888 S	75.00	90.00	135.00
7,565	1889	200.00	300.00	750.00
4,328	1890	250.00	350.00	900.00
53,800	1890 CC	100.00	150.00	400.00
61,413	1891	75.00	100.00	300.00
208,000	1891 CC	100.00	150.00	400.00
753,572	1892	75.00	85.00	120.00
82,968	1892 CC	100.00	160.00	400.00
10,000	1892 O	400.00	600.00	1750.00
298,400	1892 S	75.00	85.00	135.00
1,528,197	1893	75.00	85.00	120.00
60,000	1893 CC	100.00	160.00	400.00
110,000	1893 O	125.00	165.00	450.00
224,000	1893 S	75.00	85.00	135.00
957,955	1894	75.00	85.00	135.00
16,600	1894 O	135.00	185.00	500.00
55,900	1894 S	70.00	85.00	175.00
1,345,936	1895	75.00	85.00	120.00
112,000	1895 S	70.00	85.00	175.00
59,063	1896	75.00	90.00	175.00
155,400	1896 S	75.00	85.00	135.00
867,883	1897	75.00	85.00	125.00
354,000	1897 S	75.00	85.00	125.00
633,495	1898	75.00	85.00	125.00
1,397,400	1898 S	75.00	85.00	125.00
1,710,729	1899	75.00	85.00	125.00
1,545,000	1899 S	75.00	85.00	125.00
1,405,730	1900	75.00	85.00	120.00
329,000	1900 S	75.00	85.00	120.00
616,400	1901	75.00	85.00	120.00
3,648,000	1901 S	75.00	85.00	120.00
172,562	1902	75.00	85.00	120.00
939,000	1902 S	75.00	85.00	120.00
227,024	1903	75.00	85.00	120.00
1,855,000	1903 S	75.00	85.00	120.00
392,136	1904	75.00	85.00	120.00
97,000	1904 S	80.00	100.00	275.00
302,308	1905	75.00	85.00	120.00
880,700	1905 S	75.00	85.00	120.00
348,820	1906	75.00	85.00	120.00
320,000	1906 D	75.00	85.00	150.00

Coronet Type With Motto

Quantity	Year	Fine	Very Fine	Unc.
598,000	1906 S	$75.00	$85.00	$120.00
626,192	1907	75.00	85.00	120.00
888,000	1907 D	75.00	85.00	150.00
421,874	1908	75.00	85.00	125.00

Indian Head Incuse Type

The mint mark is to the left of the eagle's claw on the reverse.

Quantity	Year	Fine	Very Fine	Unc.
578,012	1908	80.00	95.00	325.00
148,000	1908 D	80.00	95.00	325.00
82,000	1908 S	125.00	225.00	1500.00
627,138	1909	80.00	95.00	325.00
3,423,560	1909 D	80.00	95.00	325.00
34,200	1909 O rare	250.00	425.00	4000.00
297,200	1909 S	80.00	110.00	600.00
604,250	1910	80.00	95.00	325.00
193,600	1910 D	80.00	120.00	450.00
770,200	1910 S	80.00	100.00	375.00
915,139	1911	80.00	95.00	325.00
72,500	1911 D	125.00	200.00	2000.00
1,416,000	1911 S	80.00	100.00	500.00
790,144	1912	80.00	95.00	325.00
392,000	1912 S	80.00	110.00	325.00
916,099	1913	80.00	95.00	325.00
408,000	1913 S	100.00	120.00	850.00
247,125	1914	80.00	100.00	325.00
247,000	1914 D	80.00	100.00	375.00
263,000	1914 S	80.00	100.00	435.00
588,075	1915	80.00	95.00	325.00
164,000	1915 S	100.00	125.00	850.00
240,000	1916 S	100.00	125.00	750.00
662,000	1929 rare	1250.00	1500.00	4500.00

Eagles ($10)

No value appeared on these coins until 1838.

The eagles and double eagles first issued in 1907 were designed by the distinguished sculptor, Augustus Saint-Gaudens. They are generally considered the most beautiful of all United States coins. Theodore Roosevelt, who was President at the time, forbade the use of the motto "In God We Trust" on these coins. He felt that the appearance of this phrase on a coin was in bad taste. His successor, President Taft, had the motto restored in 1908.

EAGLES ($10 GOLD PIECES)

Bust Type

1795-1797   1797-1804

Quantity	Year	Fine	Very Fine	Unc.
2,795	1795	$2500.00	$3500.00	$15,000.00
6,080	1796	2000.00	3500.00	12,000.00
9,177 {	1797 small eagle	2750.00	3500.00	16,000.00
	1797 large eagle	1100.00	1600.00	6000.00
7,974 {	1798 over 97; 4 stars before bust	2000.00	2750.00	8500.00
	1798 over 97; 6 stars before bust	5500.00	13,000.00	30,000.00
17,483	1799	1200.00	2000.00	5000.00
25,965	1800	1500.00	2000.00	6500.00
29,254	1801	1200.00	2000.00	5000.00
8,979	1803	1300.00	2000.00	6000.00
9,795	1804	2000.00	3250.00	9500.00

EAGLES (continued)

Coronet Type

1838-1865   1866-1907

The mint mark is below the eagle on the reverse.

Quantity	Year	Very Fine	Ext. Fine	Unc.
27,200	1838	$1250.00	$2000.00	$4000.00
32,248	1839	850.00	1500.00	3500.00
47,338	1840	200.00	275.00	1500.00
63,131	1841	200.00	250.00	1400.00
2,500	1841 O	550.00	850.00	2750.00
81,507	1842	175.00	250.00	1300.00
27,400	1842 O	200.00	275.00	1500.00
75,462	1843	175.00	250.00	1200.00
175,162	1843 O	175.00	250.00	1200.00
6,361	1844	400.00	750.00	2500.00
118,700	1844 O	175.00	235.00	1000.00
26,153	1845	200.00	300.00	1500.00
47,500	1845 O	175.00	250.00	1400.00
20,095	1846	200.00	300.00	1500.00
81,780	1846 O	175.00	250.00	1350.00
862,258	1847	165.00	225.00	950.00
571,500	1847 O	175.00	250.00	1400.00
145,484	1848	165.00	225.00	1100.00
35,850	1848 O	185.00	250.00	1450.00
653,618	1849	165.00	225.00	950.00
23,900	1849 O	200.00	300.00	1700.00
291,451	1850	165.00	225.00	950.00
57,500	1850 O	185.00	250.00	1200.00
176,328	1851	165.00	225.00	950.00
263,000	1851 O	175.00	250.00	1250.00
263,106	1852	165.00	225.00	950.00
18,000	1852 O	250.00	400.00	1800.00
201,253	1853	175.00	225.00	950.00
51,000	1853 O	200.00	250.00	1450.00
54,250	1854	185.00	250.00	1250.00
52,500	1854 O	250.00	350.00	1500.00
123,826	1854 S	225.00	350.00	1200.00
121,701	1855	175.00	225.00	950.00
18,000	1855 O	250.00	450.00	1800.00
9,000	1855 S	325.00	500.00	2250.00
60,490	1856	185.00	250.00	1100.00
14,500	1856 O	250.00	375.00	1750.00
68,000	1856 S	250.00	350.00	1400.00
16,606	1857	250.00	350.00	1800.00
5,500	1857 O	575.00	850.00	3250.00
26,000	1857 S	250.00	350.00	1650.00
2,521	1858 ext. rare	4500.00	6000.00	9000.00
20,000	1858 O	275.00	400.00	1650.00
11,800	1858 S	300.00	475.00	2000.00

111

EAGLES (continued)

Quantity	Year	Very Fine	Ext. Fine	Unc.
	Coronet Type			
16,093	1859	$250.00	$350.00	$1750.00
2,300	1859 O	1500.00	2500.00	3500.00
7,000	1859 S	500.00	800.00	2200.00
11,783	1860	225.00	350.00	1600.00
11,100	1860 O	350.00	600.00	2000.00
5,000	1860 S	600.00	850.00	2750.00
113,233	1861	185.00	225.00	1100.00
15,500	1861 S	250.00	500.00	1800.00
10,995	1862	300.00	400.00	1800.00
12,500	1862 S	375.00	800.00	2000.00
1,248	1863	2500.00	3500.00	9000.00
10,000	1863 S	500.00	750.00	3000.00
3,580	1864	750.00	1200.00	3500.00
2,500	1864 S	2000.00	3000.00	5000.00
4,005	1865	750.00	1000.00	3000.00
16,700	1865 S	800.00	1250.00	3000.00
20,000*	1866 S	850.00	1200.00	2500.00

Coronet Type With Motto
The mint mark is below the eagle on the reverse.

Quantity	Year	Very Fine	Ext. Fine	Unc.
3,780	1866	$450.00	$750.00	$1200.00
*	1866 S	350.00	500.00	1200.00
3,140	1867	450.00	725.00	1100.00
9,000	1867 S	350.00	500.00	1000.00
10,655	1868	300.00	400.00	800.00
13,500	1868 S	300.00	400.00	800.00
1,855	1869	1200.00	2250.00	4000.00
6,430	1869 S	350.00	500.00	1100.00
2,535	1870	500.00	700.00	1250.00
5,908	1870 CC	850.00	1750.00	2500.00
8,000	1870 S	375.00	500.00	1000.00
1,780	1871	1100.00	1700.00	3500.00
7,185	1871 CC	750.00	1250.00	2000.00
16,500	1871 S	275.00	375.00	750.00
1,650	1872	1000.00	1500.00	3000.00
5,500	1872 CC	750.00	1250.00	2500.00
17,300	1872 S	250.00	350.00	750.00
825	1873	2000.00	2500.00	5000.00
4,543	1873 CC	1500.00	3000.00	5000.00
12,000	1873 S	300.00	400.00	800.00
53,160	1874	185.00	250.00	350.00
16,767	1874 CC	400.00	600.00	1250.00
10,000	1874 S	250.00	350.00	750.00
120	1875 rare	10,500.00		
7,715	1875 CC	600.00	1000.00	1500.00
732	1876	1750.00	2500.00	5000.00
4,696	1876 CC	1250.00	1750.00	3500.00
5,000	1876 S	650.00	850.00	1500.00
817	1877	1750.00	2500.00	5000.00
3,332	1877 CC	1250.00	1750.00	3500.00
17,000	1877 S	175.00	225.00	3500.00
73,800	1878	175.00	200.00	250.00
3,244	1878 CC	1250.00	1750.00	3750.00
26,100	1878 S	165.00	185.00	275.00
384,770	1879	165.00	185.00	225.00
1,762	1879 CC	5000.00	7500.00	10,000.00
1,500	1879 O	1750.00	2500.00	5000.00
224,000	1879 S	165.00	175.00	225.00
1,644,876	1880	165.00	175.00	215.00
11,190	1880 CC	250.00	375.00	550.00
9,200	1880 O	200.00	300.00	500.00
506,250	1880 S	165.00	175.00	215.00

* Includes 1866 S coins with motto.

Quantity	Year	Very Fine	Ext. Fine	Unc.
		Coronet Type Without Motto		
3,877,260	1881	$165.00	$175.00	$215.00
24,015	1881 CC	200.00	300.00	500.00
8,350	1881 O	200.00	300.00	600.00
970,000	1881 S	165.00	175.00	225.00
2,324,480	1882	145.00	160.00	190.00
6,764	1882 CC	275.00	500.00	1000.00
10,820	1882 O	200.00	250.00	400.00
132,000	1882 S	165.00	175.00	225.00
208,740	1883	165.00	175.00	225.00
12,000	1883 CC	200.00	275.00	500.00
800	1883 O rare	2500.00	3500.00	6500.00
38,000	1883 S	175.00	225.00	350.00
76,905	1884	165.00	190.00	250.00
9,925	1884 CC	225.00	300.00	750.00
124,250	1884 S	165.00	175.00	225.00
253,527	1885	145.00	165.00	200.00
228,000	1885 S	145.00	165.00	200.00
236,160	1886	145.00	165.00	200.00
826,000	1886 S	145.00	165.00	190.00
53,680	1887	175.00	195.00	250.00
817,000	1887 S	145.00	165.00	190.00
132,996	1888	145.00	165.00	200.00
21,335	1888 O	175.00	225.00	375.00
648,700	1888 S	145.00	165.00	190.00
4,485	1889	375.00	575.00	1000.00
425,400	1889 S	145.00	165.00	190.00
58,043	1890	160.00	175.00	250.00
17,500	1890 CC	200.00	275.00	450.00
91,868	1891	160.00	190.00	250.00
103,732	1891 CC	175.00	225.00	375.00
797,552	1892	145.00	165.00	190.00
40,000	1892 CC	200.00	250.00	400.00
28,688	1892 O	185.00	225.00	325.00
115,500	1892 S	145.00	165.00	225.00
1,840,895	1893	145.00	165.00	190.00
14,000	1893 CC	185.00	250.00	450.00
17,000	1893 O	175.00	250.00	500.00
141,350	1893 S	145.00	165.00	200.00
2,470,778	1894	145.00	165.00	190.00
107,500	1894 O	165.00	185.00	250.00
25,000	1894 S	175.00	200.00	350.00
567,826	1895	145.00	165.00	190.00
98,000	1895 O	165.00	185.00	250.00
49,000	1895 S	160.00	175.00	250.00
76,348	1896	160.00	190.00	250.00
123,750	1896 S	145.00	165.00	200.00
1,000,159	1897	145.00	165.00	190.00
42,500	1897 O	165.00	185.00	300.00
234,750	1897 S	145.00	165.00	190.00
812,197	1898	145.00	165.00	190.00
473,600	1898 S	145.00	165.00	190.00
1,262,305	1899	145.00	165.00	190.00
37,047	1899 O	165.00	225.00	375.00
841,000	1899 S	145.00	165.00	190.00
293,960	1900	145.00	165.00	190.00
81,000	1900 S	150.00	175.00	250.00
1,718,825	1901	145.00	165.00	215.00
72,041	1901 O	165.00	185.00	275.00
2,812,750	1901 S	145.00	165.00	190.00
82,513	1902	165.00	190.00	250.00
469,500	1902 S	145.00	165.00	190.00
125,926	1903	145.00	165.00	200.00
112,771	1903 O	165.00	185.00	275.00

Quantity	Year	Very Fine	Ext. Fine	Unc.
	Coronet Type Without Motto			
538,000	1903 S	$145.00	$165.00	$190.00
162,038	1904	145.00	165.00	190.00
108,950	1904 O	165.00	185.00	275.00
201,087	1905	145.00	165.00	190.00
369,250	1905 S	160.00	180.00	225.00
165,497	1906	145.00	165.00	200.00
981,000	1906 D	145.00	165.00	190.00
86,895	1906 O	175.00	195.00	275.00
457,000	1906 S	160.00	175.00	225.00
1,203,973	1907	145.00	165.00	190.00
1,030,000	1907 D	145.00	165.00	190.00
210,500	1907 S	160.00	175.00	225.00

Indian Head Type

Without Motto   With Motto

The mint mark is to the left of the eagle's claw on the reverse.

Quantity	Year	Very Fine	Ext. Fine	Unc.
500	1907 Periods before and after legends. Wire edge			7500.00
42	1907 As above, but with rolled edge			30,000.00
239,406	1907 No periods	225.00	325.00	750.00
33,500	1908 No motto	350.00	550.00	1850.00
210,000	1908 D No motto	225.00	325.00	800.00
341,486	1908 Motto	185.00	225.00	425.00
836,500	1908 D Motto	185.00	225.00	425.00
59,850	1908 S	300.00	550.00	2000.00
184,863	1909	185.00	225.00	450.00
121,540	1909 D	185.00	225.00	475.00
292,350	1909 S	200.00	235.00	450.00
318,704	1910	185.00	225.00	425.00
2,356,640	1910 D	185.00	225.00	425.00
811,000	1910 S	185.00	250.00	550.00
505,595	1911	185.00	225.00	425.00
30,100	1911 D	400.00	750.00	3000.00
51,000	1911 S	300.00	400.00	1250.00
405,083	1912	185.00	225.00	425.00
300,000	1912 S	185.00	250.00	550.00
442,071	1913	185.00	225.00	425.00
66,000	1913 S	300.00	525.00	1000.00
151,050	1914	185.00	225.00	425.00
343,500	1914 D	185.00	225.00	425.00
208,000	1914 S	190.00	250.00	500.00
351,075	1915	185.00	225.00	425.00
59,000	1915 S	275.00	375.00	1100.00
138,000	1916 S	275.00	375.00	850.00
126,500	1920 S	5500.00	8500.00	22,000.00
1,014,000	1926	185.00	225.00	325.00
96,000	1930 S	3000.00	4000.00	8000.00
4,463,000	1932	185.00	225.00	325.00
312,500	1933		7500.00	35,000.00

Double Eagles ($20)

This denomination, the highest in American coinage, made its appearance when gold became plentiful after the discovery of gold in California.

The rarest double eagle is that of 1849. Only one was issued and it is in the collection of the United States Mint.

DOUBLE EAGLES ($20 GOLD PIECES)
Coronet Type

Without Motto
1850-1865

With Motto
1866-1907

The mint mark is below the eagle on the reverse.

Quantity	Year	Very Fine	Ext. Fine	Unc.
1,170,261	1850	$500.00	$650.00	$3000.00
141,000	1850 O	600.00	1000.00	3500.00
2,087,155	1851	350.00	400.00	2200.00
315,000	1851 O	450.00	1000.00	2250.00
2,053,026	1852	350.00	400.00	1750.00
190,000	1852 O	450.00	1000.00	2500.00
1,261,326	1853	350.00	400.00	1750.00
71,000	1853 O	450.00	1000.00	2500.00
757,899	1854	350.00	400.00	1750.00
3,250	1854 O		12,000.00	
141,468	1854 S	400.00	550.00	2250.00
364,666	1855	350.00	400.00	2000.00
8,000	1855 O	1250.00	1750.00	4500.00
879,675	1855 S	350.00	400.00	1750.00
329,878	1856	350.00	400.00	1750.00
2,250	1856 O		8500.00	
1,189,750	1856 S	350.00	400.00	1500.00
439,375	1857	350.00	400.00	1500.00
30,000	1857 O	500.00	700.00	2250.00
970,500	1857 S	350.00	400.00	1500.00
211,714	1858	350.00	400.00	1750.00
32,250	1858 O	600.00	1000.00	3500.00
846,710	1858 S	350.00	400.00	1750.00
43,597	1859	400.00	500.00	2000.00
9,100	1859 O	1300.00	2000.00	5000.00
636,445	1859 S	350.00	425.00	1500.00
577,670	1860	350.00	400.00	1750.00
6,600	1860 O	2000.00	3500.00	5000.00
544,950	1860 S	350.00	425.00	1500.00
2,976,453	1861	350.00	425.00	1500.00
5,000	1861 O	1100.00	2000.00	4500.00
768,000	1861 S	350.00	425.00	1500.00

Quantity	Year	Very Fine	Ext. Fine	Unc.
	Coronet Type			
?	1861 S Paquet's reverse (an outstanding rarity)			
92,133	1862	$400.00	$600.00	$1750.00
854,173	1862 S	350.00	425.00	1650.00
142,790	1863	375.00	500.00	1850.00
966,570	1863 S	350.00	425.00	1650.00
204,285	1864	375.00	475.00	1650.00
793,660	1864 S	350.00	425.00	1750.00
351,200	1865	375.00	475.00	1750.00
1,042,500	1865 S	350.00	425.00	1750.00
?	1866 S No motto	700.00	1250.00	3000.00
698,775	1866	315.00	375.00	1250.00
842,250	1866 S	315.00	375.00	1000.00
251,065	1867	315.00	375.00	1000.00
920,750	1867 S	315.00	350.00	900.00
98,000	1868	325.00	375.00	1000.00
837,500	1868 S	315.00	350.00	900.00
175,155	1869	315.00	375.00	850.00
686,750	1869 S	315.00	350.00	850.00
155,185	1870	315.00	375.00	850.00
3,789	1870 CC		20,000.00	
982,000	1870 S	315.00	350.00	1250.00
80,150	1871	325.00	375.00	950.00
14,687	1871 CC	1750.00	2500.00	3500.00
928,000	1871 S	315.00	350.00	600.00
251,880	1872	325.00	375.00	750.00
29,650	1872 CC	600.00	1250.00	2500.00
780,000	1872 S	315.00	350.00	600.00
1,709,825	1873	315.00	350.00	600.00
22,410	1873 CC	600.00	1000.00	2250.00
1,040,600	1873 S	315.00	350.00	600.00
366,800	1874	315.00	350.00	650.00
115,085	1874 CC	375.00	450.00	1000.00
1,214,000	1874 S	315.00	350.00	600.00
295,740	1875	315.00	350.00	650.00
111,151	1875 CC	375.00	450.00	1000.00
1,230,000	1875 S	315.00	350.00	600.00
583,905	1876	315.00	350.00	600.00
138,441	1876 CC	400.00	425.00	1200.00
1,597,000	1876 S	315.00	350.00	600.00
397,670	1877	300.00	325.00	375.00
42,565	1877 CC	400.00	500.00	1500.00
1,735,000	1877 S	300.00	325.00	360.00
543,645	1878	300.00	325.00	360.00
13,180	1878 CC	550.00	975.00	2500.00
1,739,000	1878 S	300.00	325.00	360.00
207,630	1879	300.00	325.00	375.00
10,708	1879 CC	650.00	1500.00	3000.00
2,325	1879 O	2250.00	3500.00	7500.00
1,223,800	1879 S	300.00	325.00	360.00
51,456	1880	315.00	350.00	475.00
836,000	1880 S	300.00	325.00	360.00
2,260	1881	3000.00	5000.00	10,000.00
727,000	1881 S	300.00	325.00	360.00
630	1882 rare	2750.00	5000.00	12,000.00
39,140	1882 CC	450.00	550.00	1250.00
1,125,000	1882 S	300.00	325.00	360.00
40	1883 very rare (only proofs were struck)			20,000.00
59,962	1883 CC	350.00	500.00	1250.00
1,189,000	1883 S	300.00	325.00	360.00
71	1884 very rare (only proofs were struck)			
81,139	1884 CC	375.00	500.00	1000.00
916,000	1884 S	300.00	325.00	360.00

Quantity	Year	Very Fine	Ext. Fine	Unc.
	Coronet Type			
828	1885	$2250.00	$3500.00	$9000.00
9,450	1885 CC	575.00	1250.00	2100.00
683,500	1885 S	300.00	325.00	360.00
1,106	1886	3000.00	5000.00	10,000.00
121	1887 rare (only proofs were struck)			
283,000	1887 S	300.00	330.00	400.00
226,266	1888	300.00	330.00	450.00
859,600	1888 S	300.00	325.00	375.00
44,111	1889	300.00	350.00	600.00
30,945	1889 CC	350.00	425.00	1250.00
774,700	1889 S	300.00	325.00	360.00
75,995	1890	300.00	330.00	450.00
91,209	1890 CC	350.00	475.00	1000.00
802,750	1890 S	300.00	325.00	360.00
1,442	1891	2000.00	3000.00	7500.00
5,000	1891 CC	1750.00	2500.00	5500.00
1,288,125	1891 S	275.00	300.00	325.00
4,523	1892	1000.00	1500.00	5000.00
27,265	1892 CC	500.00	600.00	1500.00
930,150	1892 S	275.00	300.00	325.00
344,339	1893	300.00	325.00	400.00
18,402	1893 CC	600.00	750.00	2000.00
996,175	1893 S	275.00	300.00	325.00
1,368,990	1894	275.00	300.00	325.00
1,048,550	1894 S	275.00	300.00	325.00
1,114,656	1895	275.00	300.00	325.00
1,143,500	1895 S	275.00	300.00	325.00
792,663	1896	275.00	300.00	325.00
1,403,925	1896 S	275.00	300.00	325.00
1,383,261	1897	275.00	300.00	325.00
1,470,250	1897 S	275.00	300.00	325.00
170,470	1898	300.00	330.00	400.00
2,575,175	1898 S	275.00	300.00	325.00
1,669,384	1899	275.00	300.00	325.00
2,010,300	1899 S	275.00	300.00	325.00
1,874,584	1900	275.00	300.00	325.00
2,459,500	1900 S	275.00	300.00	325.00
111,526	1901	300.00	330.00	400.00
1,596,000	1901 S	275.00	300.00	325.00
31,254	1902	325.00	375.00	600.00
1,753,625	1902 S	275.00	300.00	325.00
287,428	1903	300.00	330.00	375.00
954,000	1903 S	275.00	300.00	325.00
6,256,797	1904	275.00	300.00	325.00
5,134,175	1904 S	275.00	300.00	325.00
59,011	1905	315.00	350.00	575.00
1,813,000	1905 S	275.00	300.00	325.00
69,600	1906	315.00	350.00	575.00
620,250	1906 D	275.00	300.00	325.00
2,065,750	1906 S	275.00	300.00	325.00
1,451,864	1907	275.00	300.00	325.00
842,250	1907 D	315.00	330.00	370.00
2,165,800	1907 S	275.00	300.00	325.00

The mint mark is above the date on the reverse.

Quantity	Year		Very Fine	Ext. Fine	Unc.
16 *	1907 very high relief (ext. rare)				$42,500.00
11,250 {	1907 MCMVII date high relief with wire edge		$1400.00	$2000.00	4750.00
	1907 same with flat edge		1400.00	2000.00	4750.00

Without Motto
1907-1908

With Motto
1908-1933

Quantity	Year	Very Fine	Ext. Fine	Unc.
361,667	1907 Arabic date	300.00	325.00	400.00
4,271,551	1908 no motto	275.00	300.00	325.00
663,750	1908 D no motto	275.00	300.00	325.00
156,359	1908 motto	275.00	300.00	325.00
349,500	1908 D motto	275.00	300.00	325.00
22,000	1908 S motto	500.00	1000.00	3500.00
161,282 {	1909 over 8	325.00	400.00	600.00
	1909	300.00	325.00	400.00
52,500	1909 D	400.00	625.00	2500.00
2,774,925	1909 S	275.00	300.00	325.00
482,167	1910	275.00	300.00	325.00
429,000	1910 D	275.00	300.00	325.00
2,128,250	1910 S	275.00	300.00	325.00
197,350	1911	275.00	300.00	325.00
846,500	1911 D	275.00	300.00	325.00
775,750	1911 S	275.00	300.00	325.00
149,824	1912	315.00	335.00	420.00
168,838	1913	275.00	300.00	350.00
393,500	1913 D	275.00	300.00	325.00
34,000	1913 S	325.00	400.00	850.00

* The very high relief experimental pieces show 14 rays extending from the sun on the reverse side. The regular issue high relief coins have only 13 rays.

Quantity	Year	Very Fine	Ext. Fine	Unc.
95,320	1914	$315.00	$335.00	$385.00
453,000	1914 D	275.00	300.00	325.00
1,498,000	1914 S	275.00	300.00	325.00
152,050	1915	315.00	335.00	385.00
567,500	1915 S	275.00	300.00	325.00
796,000	1916 S	300.00	325.00	385.00
228,250	1920	300.00	325.00	350.00
558,000	1920 S	3000.00	5000.00	12,500.00
528,500	1921	6000.00	7500.00	20,000.00
1,375,500	1922	275.00	300.00	325.00
2,658,000	1922 S	350.00	500.00	750.00
566,000	1923	275.00	300.00	325.00
1,702,000	1923 D	275.00	300.00	375.00
4,323,500	1924	275.00	300.00	375.00
3,049,500	1924 D	350.00	475.00	1000.00
2,927,500	1924 S	400.00	500.00	1000.00
2,831,750	1925	300.00	325.00	375.00
2,938,500	1925 D	450.00	725.00	3000.00
3,776,500	1925 S	325.00	450.00	1200.00
816,750	1926	300.00	325.00	375.00
481,000	1926 D	600.00	900.00	2500.00
2,041,500	1926 S	350.00	500.00	1650.00
2,946,750	1927	275.00	300.00	325.00
180,000	1927 D			60,000.00
3,107,000	1927 S	1500.00	3000.00	6500.00
8,816,000	1928	275.00	300.00	325.00
1,779,750	1929	1500.00	3000.00	6500.00
74,000	1930 S		7000.00	17,500.00
2,938,250	1931		5000.00	12,000.00
106,500	1931 D		7000.00	17.500.00
1,101,750	1932		5000.00	15,000.00
445,500	1933 not officially released			

COMMEMORATIVE COINS

American commemorative coins make up the handsomest and most varied series in all our coinage. Almost all buying and selling of these coins are for the uncirculated state; the commemoratives have never been intended for general use. To date there are 50 silver commemorative coins and 10 gold commemorative coins.

Several of these coins have been issued in a considerable variety of dates and mint marks. The Texas Centennial coin, for example, has 13 such varieties. For the collector who is not a specialist, the advisable course is to limit himself to the cheapest variety of such a coin. In this way he will be able to acquire the largest number of commemorative coins.

The gold commemorative coins are of course more expensive than the silver coins which make up the bulk of the commemorative coinage. The two outstanding rarities among commemorative coins are the 1915 S Panama-Pacific $50 gold pieces.

SILVER COMMEMORATIVE COINS
(Half Dollars unless otherwise specified)

Quantity	Year	Unc.
950,000	1892 Columbian Exposition	$20.00
1,550,405	1893 Columbian Exposition	20.00
24,191	1893 Isabella Quarter	180.00
36,000	1900 Lafayette Dollar	500.00
27,134	1915 S Panama-Pacific Exposition	300.00
100,058	1918 Illinois Centennial	45.00
50,028	1920 Maine Centennial	55.00
152,112	*1920 Pilgrim Tercentenary	35.00
20,053	*1921 Pilgrim Tercentenary (1921 on obverse)	75.00
5,000	1921 Missouri Centennial (2 x 4)	525.00
15,400	1921 Missouri Centennial (no 2 x 4)	500.00
6,006	1921 Alabama Centennial (with 2 x 2)	300.00
49,038	1921 Alabama Centennial (no 2 x 2)	200.00
4,250	1922 Grant Memorial (with star)	550.00
67,411	1922 Grant Memorial (no star)	60.00
274,077	1923 S Monroe Doctrine Centennial	45.00
142,080	1924 Huguenot-Walloon Tercentenary	50.00
162,099	1925 Lexington-Concord Sesquicentennial	45.00
1,314,709	1925 Stone Mountain Memorial	22.50
86,594	1925 S California Diamond Jubilee	50.00
14,994	1925 Fort Vancouver Centennial	230.00
141,120	1926 Sesquicentennial of American Independence	45.00
48,030	1926 Oregon Trail Memorial	40.00
86,354	1926 S Oregon Trail Memorial	40.00
6,028	1928 Oregon Trail Memorial	55.00
5,008	1933 D Oregon Trail Memorial	80.00
7,006	1934 D Oregon Trail Memorial	60.00

1892 Columbian
Exposition

1920 Pilgrim
Tercentenary

* Of the total 1920-1921 issue, 148,000 coins were melted down by the Mint.

Quantity	Year	Unc.
10,006	1936 Oregon Trail Memorial	$ 50.00
5,006	1936 S Oregon Trail Memorial	70.00
12,008	1937 D Oregon Trail Memorial	45.00
6,006	1938 Oregon Trail Memorial	
6,005	1938 D Oregon Trail Memorial	
6,006	1938 S Oregon Trail Memorial	
	1938 P-D-S (set of three)	115.00
3,004	1939 Oregon Trail Memorial	
3,004	1939 D Oregon Trail Memorial	
3,005	1939 S Oregon Trail Memorial	
	1939 P-D-S (set of three)	285.00
28,142	1927 Vermont Sesquicentennial	80.00
10,008	1928 Hawaiian Sesquicentennial	1000.00
25,015	1934 Maryland Tercentenary	55.00
61,350	1934 Texas Centennial	40.00
9,994	1935 Texas Centennial	
10,007	1935 D Texas Centennial	
10,008	1935 S Texas Centennial	
	1935 P-D-S (set of three)	115.00
8,911	1936 Texas Centennial	
9,039	1936 D Texas Centennial	
9,064	1936 S Texas Centennial	
	1936 P-D-S (set of three)	115.00
6,571	1937 Texas Centennial	
6,605	1937 D Texas Centennial	
6,637	1937 S Texas Centennial	
	1937 P-D-S (set of three)	150.00
3,780	1938 Texas Centennial	
3,775	1938 D Texas Centennial	
3,816	1938 S Texas Centennial	
	1938 P-D-S (set of three)	300.00
10,007	1934 Daniel Boone Bicentennial	40.00
10,010	1935 Daniel Boone Bicentennial	
5,005	1935 D Daniel Boone Bicentennial	
5,005	1935 S Daniel Boone Bicentennial	
	1935 P-D-S (set of three)	130.00
10,008	*1935 Daniel Boone Bicentennial	
2,003	*1935 D Daniel Boone Bicentennial	
2,004	*1935 S Daniel Boone Bicentennial	
	1935 P-D-S (set of three)	850.00
12,012	1936 Daniel Boone Bicentennial	
5,005	1936 D Daniel Boone Bicentennial	
5,006	1936 S Daniel Boone Bicentennial	
	1936 P-D-S (set of three)	130.00
9,810	1937 Daniel Boone Bicentennial	
2,506	1937 D Daniel Boone Bicentennial	
2,506	1937 S Daniel Boone Bicentennial	
	1937 P-D-S (set of three)	315.00
2,100	1938 Daniel Boone Bicentennial	
2,100	1938 D Daniel Boone Bicentennial	
2,100	1938 S Daniel Boone Bicentennial	
	1938 P-D-S (set of three)	625.00
25,018	1935 Connecticut Tercentenary	110.00
13,012	1935 Arkansas Centennial	35.00
5,505	1935 D Arkansas Centennial	35.00
5,506	1935 S Arkansas Centennial	35.00
9,660	1936 Arkansas Centennial	
9,660	1936 D Arkansas Centennial	
9,662	1936 S Arkansas Centennial	
	1936 P-D-S (set of three)	110.00

* Small "1934" added on reverse.

Oregon Trail Memorial

Texas Centennial

Daniel Boone
Bicentennial

SILVER COMMEMORATIVE HALF DOLLARS (continued)

Quantity	Year	Unc.
5,505	1937 Arkansas Centennial	
5,505	1937 D Arkansas Centennial	
5,506	1937 S Arkansas Centennial	
	1937 P-D-S (set of three)	$110.00
3,156	1938 Arkansas Centennial	
3,155	1938 D Arkansas Centennial	
3,156	1938 S Arkansas Centennial	
	1938 P-D-S (set of three)	225.00
2,104	1939 Arkansas Centennial	
2,104	1939 D Arkansas Centennial	
2,105	1939 S Arkansas Centennial	
	1939 P-D-S (set of three)	630.00
10,008	1935 Hudson, N. Y. Sesquicentennial	425.00
70,132	1935 S California-Pacific Exposition	40.00
30,092	1936 D California-Pacific Exposition	50.00
10,008	1935 Old Spanish Trail	450.00
20,013	1936 Rhode Island Tercentenary	
15,010	1936 D Rhode Island Tercentenary	
15,011	1936 S Rhode Island Tercentenary	
	1936 P-D-S (set of three)	120.00
50,030	1936 Cleveland, Great Lakes Exposition	35.00
25,015	1936 Wisconsin Territorial Centennial	80.00
5,005	1936 Cincinnati Musical Center	
5,005	1936 D Cincinnati Musical Center	
5,006	1936 S Cincinnati Musical Center	
	1936 P-D-S (set of three)	575.00
81,773	1936 Long Island Tercentenary	37.50
25,015	1936 York County, Maine Tercentenary	67.50
25,015	1936 Bridgeport, Conn. Centennial	70.00
20,013	1936 Lynchburg, Va. Sesquicentennial	75.00
20,015	1936 Elgin, Illinois Centennial	82.50
16,687	1936 Albany, N. Y. Charter	135.00
71,369	1936 S San Francisco-Oakland Bay Bridge	45.00
9,007	1936 Columbia, S. C. Sesquicentennial	
8,009	1936 D Columbia, S. C. Sesquicentennial	
8,007	1936 S Columbia, S. C. Sesquicentennial	
	1936 P-D-S (set of three)	275.00
25,265	1936 Arkansas Centennial-Robinson	35.00
25,015	1936 Delaware Tercentenary	95.00
26,928	1936 Battle of Gettysburg (1863-1938)	75.00
15,000	1936 Norfolk, Va. Bicentennial	150.00
29,030	1937 Roanoke Island, N. C. (1587-1937)	50.00
18,028	1937 Battle of Antietam (1862-1937)	165.00
15,266	1938 New Rochelle, N. Y. (1688-1938)	150.00
100,057	1946 Iowa Centennial	37.50
1,000,546	1946 Booker T. Washington Memorial	7.00
200,113	1946 D Booker T. Washington Memorial	7.00
500,279	1946 S Booker T. Washington Memorial	7.00
	1946 P-D-S (set of three)	20.00
100,017	1947 Booker T. Washington Memorial	
100,017	1947 D Booker T. Washington Memorial	
100,017	1947 S Booker T. Washington Memorial	
	1947 P-D-S (set of three)	23.50
8,005	1948 Booker T. Washington Memorial	
8,005	1948 D Booker T. Washington Memorial	
8,005	1948 S Booker T. Washington Memorial	
	1948 P-D-S (set of three)	50.00
6,004	1949 Booker T. Washington Memorial	
6,004	1949 D Booker T. Washington Memorial	
6,004	1949 S Booker T. Washington Memorial	
	1949 P-D-S (set of three)	95.00

Arkansas Centennial

Old Spanish Trail

San Francisco-Oakland
Bay Bridge

Booker T. Washington
Memorial

122

SILVER COMMEMORATIVE HALF DOLLARS (continued)

Quantity	Year	Unc.
6,004	1950 Booker T. Washington Memorial	
6,004	1950 D Booker T. Washington Memorial	
512,091	1950 S Booker T. Washington Memorial	
	1950 P-D-S (set of three)	$65.00
510,082	1951 Booker T. Washington Memorial	
12,004	1951 D Booker T. Washington Memorial	
12,004	1951 S Booker T. Washington Memorial	
	1951 P-D-S (set of three)	55.00
110,018	1951 Carver-Washington	6.75
10,004	1951 D Carver-Washington	
10,004	1951 S Carver-Washington	
	1951 P-D-S (set of three)	47.50
2,006,292	1952 Carver-Washington	6.75
6,003	1952 D Carver-Washington	
6,003	1952 S Carver-Washington	
	1952 P-D-S (set of three)	45.00
8,003	1953 Carver-Washington	
8,003	1953 D Carver-Washington	
108,020	1953 S Carver-Washington	
	1953 P-D-S (set of three)	75.00
12,006	1954 Carver-Washington	
12,006	1954 D Carver-Washington	
122,024	1954 S Carver-Washington	
	1954 P-D-S (set of three)	37.50

Carver-Washington

GOLD COMMEMORATIVE COINS

Quantity	Year (*Dollars unless otherwise specified*)	Unc.
17,375	1903 Louisiana Purchase (Jefferson)	$485.00
17,375	1903 Louisiana Purchase (McKinley)	485.00
9,997	1904 Lewis and Clark Exposition	1200.00
10,000	1905 Lewis and Clark Exposition	1200.00
25,000	1915 S Panama-Pacific Exposition	350.00
6,749	1915 S Panama-Pacific Exposition ($2.50)	1750.00
483	1915 S Panama-Pacific Exposition ($50 round)	18,000.00
645	1915 S Panama-Pacific Exposition ($50 octagonal)	14,000.00
9,977	1916 McKinley Memorial	325.00
10,000	1917 McKinley Memorial	450.00
5,000	1922 Grant Memorial (with star)	975.00
5,000	1922 Grant Memorial (no star)	1000.00
46,019	1926 Philadelphia Sesquicentennial ($2.50)	300.00

1915 S Panama-Pacific
Exposition

PROOF SETS

In modern times the Mint has issued specially struck proof coins in the cent, nickel, dime, quarter, and half dollar denominations. Premium values are as follows:

1936	$1850.00	1954	$27.50	1962	$6.00
1937	800.00	1955	27.50	1963	6.00
1938	385.00	1956	12.00	1964	6.50
1939	360.00	1957	8.00	1968 S	6.00
1940	255.00	1958	12.00	1969 S	6.00
1941	245.00	1959	8.50	1970 S	6.00
1942*	285.00	1960 Large		1971 S	6.00
1950	200.00	date	7.00	1972 S	5.50
1951	145.00	1960 Small		1973 S	12.50
1952	85.00	date	25.00	1974 S	14.00
1953	55.00	1961	6.00	1975 S	

* Includes both types of nickels issued in 1942.

7. CATALOG OF U. S. TOKENS

Token collecting has long been accepted as a worth-while branch of numismatics and in many ways tokens preserve for us a more intimate picture of their times than do the coins. On tokens we find contemporary portraits of noteworthy persons as well as the slogans and sentiments of the period.

The most extensive series of American tokens appeared at the height of the Civil War in 1863-1864. They were created in response to the urgent demands of merchants for small change. These tokens, referred to at the time as "copperheads," were the size of our modern one-cent pieces.

The Civil War tokens are of two types, the storecard and the patriotic tokens. The storecard type carries the name of the merchant and his address on one side and often a representation of his product or an advertising message on the other. The patriotic tokens bear timely designs and slogans on both sides but name no place of issue.

This listing illustrates and describes the most frequently encountered types of patriotic Civil War tokens. The valuations given are for tokens in extremely fine to uncirculated condition. Uncirculated tokens retaining mint luster are worth half again as much. Specimens in much worn condition are worth considerably less. The valuations are for tokens struck on the usual copper or bronze planchets. "Off-metal" pieces of brass, nickel, copper-nickel, white metal, lead zinc, tin, German silver or coin silver are worth more to collectors who specialize in the series.

Ext. Fine-Unc.

1. Indian head, feathered headdress, stars in field.
Flags, drum, cap on pole, cannon barrels, wreath $3.50

2. Indian head, feathered headdress, stars in field
ARMY & NAVY, swords, wreath $3.50

3. Indian head, feathered headdress, stars in field.
MCCLELLAN MEDAL FOR ONE CENT $6.50

4. Indian head, feathered headdress, stars in field.
NEW YORK, wreath   5.75

5. Indian head, feathered headdress, stars in field.
NOT ONE CENT, wreath   3.50

6. Indian head, feathered headdress, stars in field
UNITED STATES OF AMERICA, eagle on shield   6.00

7. Indian head, feathered headdress, no stars in field.
NOT ONE CENT, circle of leaves 12.50

8. Indian head, feathered headdress, horseshoe of stars in field.
NOT ONE CENT, wreath $15.00

9. Indian head, feathered headdress, MILLIONS FOR CONTRACTORS.
NOT ONE CENT FOR THE WIDOWS, wreath   6.00

10. Indian head, feathered headdress, UNION AND LIBERTY.
OUR COUNTRY, circle of leaves   6.00

11. Indian head, feathered headdress, UNITED WE STAND.
UNION FOR EVER, large shield   7.50

12. Indian head, feathered crown.
OUR ARMY, wreath   3.50

125

13. Indian head, feathered
crown.
OUR ARMY, large eagle $7.50

18. Head of Liberty with cap,
facing left.
GOD PROTECT THE UNION,
wreath $7.50

14. Indian head, feathered
crown.
OUR NAVY, wreath   4.50

19. Head of Liberty with cap,
facing left.
IN REMEMBRANCE OF THE
WAR OF 1861, '62, '63   12.50

15. Indian head, feathered
crown.
UNION FOR EVER, shield   4.00

20. Head of Liberty with cap,
facing left.
I.O.U. ONE CENT, wreath   7.50

21. Head of Liberty with cap,
facing left.
MILLIONS FOR DEFENSE—NOT
ONE CENT FOR TRIBUTE,
wreath   5.50

16. Head of Liberty with cap,
facing left.
Flags, drum, cap on pole,
cannon barrels   6.75

17. Head of Liberty with cap,
facing left.
ARMY & NAVY, wreath,
swords   3.00

22. Head of Liberty with cap,
facing left.
NEW YORK, wreath   6.00

23. Head of Liberty with cap,
    facing left.
    NOT ONE CENT, wreath $6.00

24. Head of Liberty with cap,
    facing left.
    1 WILSON'S MEDAL, wreath   7.50

25. Head of Liberty with cap,
    facing left.
    OUR COUNTRY, small shield,
    circle of leaves   4.50

26. Head of Liberty with cap,
    facing left.
    PEACE FOREVER, clasped
    hands, wreath   5.50

27. Head of Liberty with cap,
    facing left.
    UNION FOR EVER, wreath,
    swords   4.50

28. Head of Liberty with cap,
    facing left, FOR PUBLIC
    ACCOMODATION.
    HORRORS OF WAR—BLESSINGS
    OF PEACE, face $6.50

29. Head of Liberty with cap,
    facing left, FOR PUBLIC
    ACCOMODATION.
    KNICKERBOCKER CURRENCY,
    man with walking stick   5.50

30. Head of Liberty with cap,
    facing left, FOR PUBLIC
    ACCOMODATION.
    UNITED STATES COPPER, eagle
    standing on globe   4.50

31. Head of Liberty with cap,
    facing right.
    OUR NAVY, wreath   6.00

32. Head of Liberty with cap,
    facing right, LIBERTY.
    Flags, drum, cap on pole,
    cannon barrels, wreath   5.50

33. Head of Liberty with cap, facing right, LIBERTY. Large shield, stars $6.50

38. Head of Liberty with coronet, facing left. UNION, eagle $6.50

34. Head of Liberty with cap, facing right, LIBERTY. OUR ARMY, circle of leaves 4.50

39. Head of Liberty with coronet, facing left, UNION. OUR CARD, wreath 5.50

35. Head of Liberty with cap, facing right, UNITED WE STAND—DIVIDED WE FALL. ARMY & NAVY, wreath, swords 4.00

40. Head of Liberty, facing right. MILLIONS FOR DEFENSE—NOT ONE CENT FOR TRIBUTE, wreath 6.00

36. Head of Liberty with turban, facing left, LIBERTY AND NO SLAVERY. Shield, flags, cap on pole, stars and wreath 6.00

41. Washington, large bust. Shield, flags, cap on pole, stars and wreath 15.00

37. Head of Liberty with turban, facing left, LIBERTY AND NO SLAVERY. UNION FOR EVER, small shield, wreath 6.00

42. Washington, large bust. NEW YORK, wreath 10.00

43. Washington, large bust.
NO COMPROMISE WITH TRAITORS, wreath $10.00

48. Washington, small bust, crossed branches.
Six-pointed star, wreath $12.50

44. Washington, large bust.
1 WILSON'S MEDAL, wreath   10.00

49. Washington, miniature bust on large star.
NOT ONE CENT, wreath   20.00

45. Washington, large bust.
UNION FOR EVER, wreath, small shield   12.50

50. Andrew Jackson, military bust, FOR OUR COUNTRY—A COMMON CAUSE.
NOW AND FOR EVER   6.50

46. Washington, small bust, crossed flags.
EXCHANGE, wreath   10.00

51. Andrew Jackson, military bust, THE UNION MUST AND SHALL BE PRESERVED.
BEWARE, curled rope snake   6.50

47. Washington, small bust, crossed flags.
PEACE FOREVER, clasped hands   7.50

52. Andrew Jackson, military bust, THE UNION MUST AND SHALL BE PRESERVED.
THIS MEDAL—PRICE ONE CENT, wreath   7.50

53. Lincoln bust, facing right.
   LINCOLN AND UNION $20.00

54. Lincoln head, facing left.
   O.K., chain of 13 links   30.00

55. Lincoln head, facing left,
   THE RIGHT MAN IN THE RIGHT
   PLACE.
   FREEDOM, wreath, small
   shield and flags   30.00

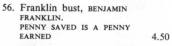

56. Franklin bust, BENJAMIN
   FRANKLIN.
   PENNY SAVED IS A PENNY
   EARNED   4.50

57. Douglas, STEPHEN A.
   DOUGLAS.
   Warrior with shield and
   spear, wreath   20.00

58. McClellan, large military
   bust, GENERAL G. B.
   McCLELLAN.
   HORRORS OF WAR—BLESSINGS
   OF PEACE, face $7.50

59. McClellan, large military
   bust, GENERAL G. B.
   McCLELLAN.
   KNICKERBOCKER CURRENCY,
   man with walking stick   6.00

60. McClellan, large military
   bust, GENERAL G. B.
   McCLELLAN.
   UNITED STATES COPPER, eagle
   standing on globe   5.50

61. McClellan, military bust,
   GEO. B. McCLELLAN.
   ARMY & NAVY, wreath   15.00

62. McClellan, small military
   bust, wreath, LITTLE MACK.
   McCLELLAN MEDAL FOR ONE
   CENT   12.50

63. McClellan, bust facing right,
THIS MEDAL OF G. B.
MCCLELLAN PRICE.
ONE CENT, wreath, shield at
top $15.00

68. Monitor, stars in field.
OUR NAVY, wreath $10.00

64. Equestrian statue of Wash-
ington, FIRST IN WAR, FIRST
IN PEACE.
THE UNION MUST AND SHALL
BE PRESERVED—JACKSON   10.00

69. Monitor, stars in field.
UNION FOR EVER, large
shield   10.00

65. Equestrian statue of Washington, FIRST IN WAR, FIRST
IN PEACE.
UNION FOR EVER, wreath,
shield   3.50

70. Monitor, OUR LITTLE MON-
ITOR.
1863, wreath, cannon bar-
rels, anchor   7.50

66. Mounted rider, horse rear-
ing, THE FEDERAL UNION IT
MUST BE PRESERVED.
OUR UNION, wreath, shield   4.50

71. Flag on pole, THE FLAG OF
OUR UNION.
ARMY & NAVY, wreath   5.50

67. Rider with sword on gallop-
ing horse.
UNION FOR EVER, large
shield   6.00

72. Flag on pole, THE FLAG OF
OUR UNION.
IF ANYBODY ATTEMPTS TO
TEAR IT DOWN—SHOOT HIM
ON THE SPOT—DIX   4.50

72a. Flag on pole, THE FLAG OF
OUR UNION.
IF ANYBODY ATTEMPTS TO
TEAR IT DOWN—SHOOT HIM
ON THE SPOOT (error)—DIX $15.00

77. Capitol building, UNITED
STATES.
ARMY & NAVY, wreath $6.00

73. Flag on pole, THE FLAG OF
OUR UNION.
THE UNION—IT MUST AND
SHALL BE PRESERVED—
JACKSON   12.50

78. Beehive, INDUSTRY.
NOT ONE CENT, wreath   7.50

74. Cannon, cannon balls, stars.
ARMY & NAVY, wreath   11.00

79. Walking man, MONEY MAKES
THE MARE GO—GO IT
BUTTONS.
KNICKERBOCKER CURRENCY,
man with walking stick   6.00

75. Cannon, PEACEMAKER.
STAND BY THE FLAG, flag on
pole   11.00

80. Walking man, MONEY MAKES
THE MARE GO—GO IT
BUTTONS.
UNITED STATES COPPER, eagle
standing on globe   6.00

76. Cannon, flag on pole, THE
PEACEMAKER.
C.L.R., wreath   15.00

81. Walking figure with sword
and flag, ornate circle.
ARMY & NAVY, wreath   7.50

82. Masonic square and compass, G.
UNION FOR EVER, wreath　$30.00

87. Eagle on shield, streamers, UNITED STATES OF AMERICA.
NOT ONE CENT, wreath　$3.50

83. Star, shield, PRO BONO PUBLICO.
NEW YORK, wreath　4.50

88. Eagle on shield, flags, branches.
NO COMPROMISE WITH TRAITORS, wreath　4.50

84. Large shield, OUR UNION.
NO COMPROMISE WITH TRAITORS, wreath　6.00

89. Eagle on shield, flags, branches.
ARMY & NAVY, wreath　3.50

85. Eagle on cannon barrel, LIBERTY FOR ALL.
AMERICA, stars, wreath　12.50

90. Flags, drum, cap on pole, cannon barrels, wreath.
Eagle on shield, flags, branches　3.50

86. Eagle, shield on breast, UNION.
THE UNION MUST AND SHALL BE PRESERVED—JACKSON　12.50

91. Flags, drum, cap on pole, cannon barrels, wreath.
ARMY & NAVY, wreath　3.50

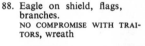

133

92. Flags, drum, cap on pole,
cannon barrels, wreath.
OUR COUNTRY, small shield,
wreath $3.50

97. REMEMBRANCE OF 1863.
ONE COUNTRY, wreath $3.50

93. Flags, drum, cap on pole,
cannon barrels, wreath.
OUR NAVY, wreath 4.00

98. REMEMBRANCE OF 1863.
NOT ONE CENT, wreath 3.50

94. Crossed flags, rays, stars,
UNION.
Six-pointed star, rays,
wreath 10.00

99. CONSTITUTION FOR EVER.
NOT ONE CENT, wreath 3.50

95. ARMY & NAVY, wreath.
THE FEDERAL UNION—IT
MUST AND SHALL BE PRE-
SERVED 3.50

100. CONSTITUTION FOR EVER.
ERINNERUNG AN 1863 4.00

96. LIBERTY 1863, wreath.
UNION, wreath 4.00

101. ERINNERUNG AN 1863.
NOT ONE CENT, wreath 6.00

102. GOOD FOR 1 CENT.
KNICKERBOCKER CURRENCY,
man with walking stick $3.50

105. I.O.U. 1 CENT, PURE COPPER.
UNITED STATES COPPER,
eagle standing on globe $3.50

103. KNICKERBOCKER CURRENCY,
man with walking stick.
UNION FOR EVER, eagle
standing on globe   3.50

106. UNITED STATES COPPER,
eagle standing on globe.
TRADESMEN'S CURRENCY,
GOOD FOR ONE CENT, out-
line of shield   3.50

104. I.O.U. 1 CENT, PURE COPPER.
KNICKERBOCKER CURRENCY,
man with walking stick   3.50

107. HORRORS OF WAR—BLES-
SINGS OF PEACE, face.
UNION FOR EVER, eagle
standing on globe   4.50

135

8. CATALOG OF CANADIAN COINS

In recent years there has been a steadily growing interest in collecting Canadian coins.

The coinage of Canada is much less ramified than United States coinage. The Province of Canada had its first coinage in 1858, and the Dominion's issues began in 1870.

These coins have always carried the portrait of the reigning British monarch on the obverse. So far five rulers have been featured:

Victoria	1858-1901
Edward VII	1902-1910
George V	1911-1936
George VI	1937-1952
Elizabeth II	1953 to date

Up to 1948, the monarch's title read *Rex et Ind: Imp* ("King and Emperor of India"). In Victoria's reign the legend read *Regina et Ind: Imp* for "Queen and Empress of India." In 1948 *et Ind: Imp* disappeared because of the change in India's status.

In Canadian coinage mint marks play a less important role than they do in United States coinage. Canadian coins have been struck at three different mints, but it has rarely happened that different mints have issued the identical denomination in the same year. Thus Canadian coinage has practically none of those sensational variations in value that come about frequently when several mints turn out coins in the same year.

As far as mint marks are concerned, Canadian coins are classified as follows:

H coins were struck at the Heaton Mint at Birmingham in England.

Coins dated between 1858 and 1907 which bear no mint mark were struck at the Royal Mint at London.

Coins dated after 1907 with the C mint mark or no mint mark were struck at the Royal Canadian Mint at Ottawa.

Two years of Canadian coinage were struck with special marks after the regular coinage for those years had already been completed. In 1937 a tiny dot was punched on the 1936 dies for the cent, 10-cent piece, and 25-cent piece. The resulting "dot" coinage resulted in the outstanding Canadian rarities as far as the cents and 10-cent coins were concerned.

In 1948 some coins were struck from the 1947 dies, with a tiny maple leaf added after the date to indicate that 1948 was the year of issue. In the tables, the notation "ML" indicates this.

In most cases, but not all, the mint reports are a useful guide to comparative scarcity. Several figures, however, are deceptive and do not give a reliable indication of scarcity. This is particularly true in regard to the following coins:

> 1875: 5 cents; 10 cents; 25 cents
> 1889: 10 cents
> 1914: 10 dollars gold
> 1921: 5 cents and 50 cents
> 1936: dot 1 cent; dot 10 cents

For many years the reverses of Canadian coins were quite plain, being limited to values and wreaths. But the first dollar, issued in 1935, was a radical departure. The first coinage of George VI in 1937 extended the change to all the other denominations. The colorful reverses that have appeared since that time place modern Canadian coins among the most picturesque and attractive coins ever issued.

The five-cent piece has gone through a number of transformations. Its silver content was dropped in 1922 in favor of nickel. During World War II nickel was needed so badly that the coin was struck in tombac brass, an alloy of 88 per cent copper and 12 per cent zinc. As this alloy is easily confused with bronze, the new coin was given a twelve-sided shape.

In 1943 the tombac was retained, but the beaver on the reverse gave way to a torch and a V for victory. This design was continued in 1944 and 1945, but chromium-finished steel replaced tombac. In 1946 nickel was again used and the beaver reappeared. However, the new coins were still twelve-sided.

In 1951 a twelve-sided nickel coin was issued to commemorate the 200th anniversary of the discovery of nickel. The beaver remained on the regular 5-cent piece, which, however, was again issued in steel because of a new nickel shortage.

CANADIAN LARGE CENTS
Province of Canada

Quantity	Year	Very Good	Fine	Very Fine	Unc.
421,000	1858	$20.00	$25.00	$35.00	$77.50
	1859	1.00	1.50	2.50	15.00
	1859 re-engraved date	12.50	17.50	22.50	55.00
9,579,000	1859 over 58, wide 9	19.50	23.50	29.50	60.00
	1859 over 58, narrow 9	25.00	35.00	45.00	90.00

Dominion of Canada

Mint marks on 1876, 1881, 1882, 1890, and 1907 issues are under date on reverse.
Mint marks on 1898 and 1900 issues are above bottom rim on reverse.

QUEEN VICTORIA

4,000,000	1876 H	1.00	1.50	2.50	12.00
2,000,000	1881 H	1.50	2.50	4.50	12.00
4,000,000	1882 H	1.00	1.50	2.50	10.00
2,500,000	1884	1.15	1.75	3.00	12.00
1,500,000	1886	1.50	2.50	4.50	17.50
1,500,000	1887	1.50	2.50	4.50	17.50
4,000,000	1888	1.00	1.50	2.00	10.00
1,000,000	1890 H	4.00	6.50	8.50	22.50
	1891 large date	4.00	6.00	8.00	20.00
1,452,537	1891 small date, small leaves	25.00	40.00	52.50	195.00
	1891 small date, large leaves	30.00	45.00	62.50	200.00
1,200,000	1892	2.50	3.50	5.00	15.00
2,000,000	1893	1.50	2.50	3.50	10.00
1,000,000	1894	6.00	8.00	10.00	25.00
1,200,000	1895	2.50	3.50	5.00	15.00
2,000,000	1896	1.00	1.50	2.25	10.00
1,500,000	1897	1.00	1.50	2.50	10.00
1,000,000	1898 H	3.25	4.50	6.50	23.50
2,400,000	1899	1.00	1.50	2.25	10.00
1,000,000	1900	5.50	7.00	9.00	25.00
2,600,000	1900 H	1.50	2.50	3.50	12.00
4,100,000	1901	.90	1.25	1.75	10.00

KING EDWARD VII

3,000,000	1902	1.10	1.50	2.50	9.00
4,000,000	1903	1.00	1.35	2.25	9.00
2,500,000	1904	1.25	2.00	3.00	10.00
2,000,000	1905	2.25	3.50	5.00	15.00
4,100,000	1906	.90	1.25	1.75	7.00
2,400,000	1907	1.25	1.75	2.50	9.00
800,000	1907 H	7.50	10.00	15.00	47.50
2,401,506	1908	1.50	2.00	3.00	9.00
3,973,329	1909	.75	1.00	1.50	6.00
5,146,487	1910	.65	.85	1.25	6.00

KING GEORGE V

4,663,486	1911	1.00	1.50	3.50	20.00
5,107,642	1912	.50	.75	1.25	5.00
5,735,405	1913	.50	.75	1.25	5.00
3,405,958	1914	.65	1.00	1.50	6.00
4,932,134	1915	.55	.85	1.25	5.00
11,022,367	1916	.30	.60	1.00	3.75
11,899,254	1917	.30	.60	1.00	3.75
12,970,798	1918	.30	.60	1.00	3.75
11,279,634	1919	.30	.60	1.00	3.75
6,762,247	1920	.35	.70	1.10	4.00

138

Quantity	Year	Very Good	Fine	Very Fine	Unc.
15,483,923	1920	$ .25	$ .40	$ .75	$6.00
7,601,627	1921	.25	.65	1.25	10.00
1,243,635	1922	7.50	9.50	14.00	100.00
1,019,002	1923	12.00	14.00	19.50	125.00
1,593,195	1924	3.00	4.50	7.00	50.00
1,000,622	1925	9.50	11.00	16.00	125.00
2,143,372	1926	2.00	2.75	3.75	25.00
3,553,928	1927	1.00	1.50	2.75	15.00
9,144,860	1928	.20	.35	.65	7.00
12,159,840	1929	.20	.35	.65	7.00
2,538,613	1930	1.50	2.00	3.00	20.00
3,842,776	1931	1.00	1.25	3.50	15.00
21,316,199	1932	.15	.25	.45	7.00
12,079,310	1933	.15	.25	.50	7.00
7,042,358	1934	.20	.30	.60	7.50
7,526,400	1935	.15	.25	.50	7.00
8,768,769	1936	.15	.25	.50	7.00
678,823	1936 dot (outstanding rarity; only 5 known)				

KING GEORGE VI

Quantity	Year			Very Fine	Unc.
10,040,231	1937			.35	2.00
18,365,608	1938			.35	2.00
21,600,319	1939			.25	1.50
85,740,532	1940			.20	1.25
56,336,011	1941			.20	3.25
76,113,708	1942			.20	4.00
89,111,969	1943			.20	1.25
44,131,216	1944			.20	1.95
77,268,591	1945			.15	.65
56,662,071	1946			.15	1.50
31,093,901	1947			.15	1.50
43,855,488	1947 ML			.15	2.00
25,767,779	1948			.15	2.75
32,190,102	1949			.10	1.25
60,444,992	1950			.10	1.00
80,430,379	1951			.10	1.25
67,633,553	1952			.10	.75

QUEEN ELIZABETH II

Quantity	Year				Unc.
72,293,723	1953				.65
21,898,646	1954				3.00
56,686,307	1955				.65
78,685,535	1956				.65
100,422,054	1957				.30
57,827,413	1958				.30
83,615,343	1959				.20
75,772,775	1960				.15
139,598,404	1961				.10
227,244,069	1962				.10
279,076,334	1963				.05
484,655,322	1964				.05
304,441,082	1965				.05
183,644,388	1966				.05
345,140,645	1967 dove reverse				.05
329,695,772	1968				.05
335,240,929	1969				.05
311,100,000	1970				.05
298,200,000	1971				.05
451,300,000	1972				.05
	1973				.05
	1974				.05
	1975				

Quantity	Year	Very Good	Fine	Very Fine	Unc.

Province of Canada

| 1,500,000 { | 1858 small date...... | $7.50 | $12.50 | $20.00 | $65.00 |
| | 1858 large date........ | 80.00 | 110.00 | 150.00 | 375.00 |

Dominion of Canada

The mint marks are below center of ribbon tying wreath on reverse.

QUEEN VICTORIA

2,800,000	1870............	6.00	8.00	11.00	55.00
1,400,000	1871............	5.00	9.00	14.00	60.00
2,000,000	1872 H	4.50	6.50	10.00	55.00
800,000	1874 H	5.00	7.50	13.50	67.50
1,000,000	1875 H	25.00	37.50	62.50	375.00
3,000,000	1880 H	2.25	3.50	7.00	50.00
1,500,000	1881 H	3.00	5.00	10.00	60.00
1,000,000	1882 H	3.00	5.00	10.00	65.00
600,000	1883 H	7.00	13.50	19.50	87.50
200,000	1884............	27.50	40.00	60.00	400.00
1,000,000	1885............	3.00	5.00	10.00	65.00
1,700,000	1886............	2.00	4.00	7.00	45.00
500,000	1887............	6.50	10.00	16.50	95.00
1,000,000	1888............	2.00	4.00	8.00	50.00
1,200,000	1889............	11.50	15.00	21.50	145.00
1,000,000	1890 H	2.00	4.00	8.00	45.00
1,800,000	1891............	2.00	4.00	7.00	40.00
860,000	1892............	3.00	5.00	8.00	50.00
1,700,000	1893............	2.00	3.00	6.00	40.00
500,000	1894............	7.50	11.00	15.00	55.00
1,500,000	1896............	2.00	3.00	6.00	35.00
1,319,283	1897............	2.00	3.00	6.00	35.00
580,717	1898............	8.00	12.00	16.00	55.00
3,000,000	1899............	1.25	2.50	3.50	30.00
1,800,000 {	1900 oval O............	1.50	3.00	4.50	30.00
	1900 round O............	11.00	17.00	27.50	80.00
2,000,000	1901............	1.50	3.00	4.50	27.00

KING EDWARD VII

2,120,000	1902............	1.00	1.25	1.75	10.00
2,200,000 {	1902 H (small H)....	7.50	10.00	15.00	30.00
	1902 H (large H)....	1.00	1.25	1.75	10.00
1,000,000	1903............	2.75	4.00	6.50	40.00
2,640,000	1903 H	1.50	2.25	3.25	20.00
2,400,000	1904............	1.50	2.25	3.25	20.00
2,600,000	1905............	1.50	2.25	3.25	20.00
3,100,000	1906............	1.25	1.75	3.00	18.00
5,200,000	1907............	1.00	1.75	3.00	18.00
1,220,524	1908............	4.00	6.00	8.50	40.00
1,983,725	1909............	1.50	3.00	4.50	25.00
5,850,325	1910............	.80	1.00	1.50	12.00

KING GEORGE V

3,692,350	1911............	1.75	3.25	5.50	50.00
5,863,170	1912............	.85	1.35	2.25	12.00
5,588,048	1913............	.85	1.35	2.25	12.00
4,202,179	1914............	.85	1.35	2.25	12.00
1,172,258	1915............	4.00	6.00	10.00	50.00
2,481,675	1916............	1.50	2.50	3.50	18.00
5,521,373	1917............	.50	.80	1.25	10.00
6,052,298	1918............	.50	.80	1.25	10.00
7,835,400	1919............	.50	.80	1.25	10.00
10,649,851	1920............	.60	.90	1.35	10.00
2,582,495	1921 rare—only about 50 known	450.00	750.00	1150.00	2750.00

Quantity	Year	Very Good	Fine	Very Fine	Unc.
	KING GEORGE V				
4,794,119	1922	$ .25	$1.00	$3.00	$50.00
2,502,279	1923	.50	1.25	4.00	70.00
3,105,839	1924	.40	1.00	3.50	60.00
201,921	1925	19.00	24.00	55.00	400.00
938,162 {	1926 Near 6	3.00	4.50	12.00	150.00
	1926 Far 6	37.50	50.00	85.00	450.00
5,285,627	1927		1.00	3.50	50.00
4,577,712	1928		1.00	3.50	50.00
5,611,911	1929		1.00	3.50	50.00
3,704,673	1930		1.00	3.50	50.00
5,100,830	1931		.75	3.00	50.00
3,198,566	1932		.75	3.00	50.00
2,597,867	1933		1.00	3.50	50.00
3,827,304	1934		.75	3.00	50.00
3,900,000	1935		.75	3.00	50.00
4,400,450	1936		.75	3.00	50.00
	KING GEORGE VI				
4,593,263	1937			1.50	20.00
3,898,974	1938			2.50	95.00
5,661,123	1939			1.50	50.00
13,920,197	1940			.75	25.00
8,681,785	1941			1.00	35.00
6,847,544	1942			.75	29.50
3,396,234	1942 tombac			1.00	3.50
24,760,256	1943 tombac			.75	3.00
11,532,784	1944 chrome steel			.50	2.25
18,893,216	1945 chrome steel			.40	1.95
6,952,684	1946			.60	7.50
7,603,724	1947			.60	7.50
9,595,124	1947 ML			.60	7.50
1,810,789	1948			2.50	17.50
12,750,002	1949			.40	5.00
4,970,520	1950			.40	5.00
8,329,321	1951 nickel commemorative			.25	2.25
4,313,410	1951 steel			.35	6.50
10,892,877	1952 steel			.25	4.00
	QUEEN ELIZABETH II				
16,638,218	1953 steel			.25	3.50
6,998,662	1954 steel			.25	7.50
5,356,020	1955 nickel			.15	5.00
9,399,854	1956 nickel				1.50
7,329,862	1957 nickel				1.50
7,592,000	1958 nickel				1.50
11,552,523	1959 nickel				.75
37,157,433	1960				.35
47,889,051	1961				.30
46,307,305	1962				.25
43,970,320	1963				.20
78,075,068	1964				.15
84,876,019	1965				.15
27,678,469	1966				.15
58,884,849	1967 rabbit reverse				.20
99,253,330	1968				.15
27,830,229	1969				.15
5,700,000	1970				.50
27,000,000	1971				.15
	1972				.10
	1973				.10
	1974				.10
	1975				

The mint marks are below center on ribbon tying wreath on reverse.

Quantity	Year	Very Good	Fine	Very Fine	Unc.
	QUEEN VICTORIA				
1,250,000	1858	$7.50	$15.00	$22.00	$135.00
1,600,000	1870	5.00	10.00	15.00	150.00
800,000	1871	7.00	14.00	23.00	160.00
1,870,000	1871 H	12.00	18.00	25.00	175.00
1,000,000	1872 H	35.00	50.00	80.00	350.00
600,000	1874 H	5.00	10.00	15.00	125.00
1,000,000	1875 H	70.00	100.00	200.00	1000.00
1,500,000	1880 H	4.00	8.00	15.00	125.00
950,000	1881 H	6.00	12.00	20.00	135.00
1,000,000	1882 H	3.00	6.50	12.50	125.00
300,000	1883 H	13.50	25.00	52.50	350.00
150,000	1884	42.50	75.00	135.00	750.00
400,000	1885	8.00	16.50	37.50	200.00
800,000	1886	7.50	15.00	30.00	155.00
350,000	1887	8.50	16.50	37.50	350.00
500,000	1888	3.00	7.50	13.50	125.00
600,000	1889	200.00	300.00	500.00	2500.00
450,000	1890 H	8.00	15.00	30.00	250.00
800,000	1891	7.50	16.50	27.50	135.00
520,000	1892	5.00	10.00	20.00	125.00
500,000 {	1893 round top 3	400.00	700.00	1000.00	7500.00
	1893 flat top 3	7.50	15.00	25.00	150.00
500,000	1894	4.00	8.00	16.50	125.00
650,000	1896	4.00	8.00	16.50	135.00
720,000	1898	4.50	9.00	18.00	125.00
1,200,000	1899	2.25	5.00	12.00	100.00
1,100,000	1900	2.00	4.50	11.00	100.00
1,200,000	1901	2.00	4.50	11.00	100.00
	KING EDWARD VII				
720,000	1902	3.00	6.00	10.00	80.00
1,100,000	1902 H	1.50	4.00	8.00	50.00
500,000	1903	5.00	10.00	20.00	125.00
1,320,000	1903 H	1.50	4.00	8.00	75.00
1,000,000	1904	5.00	10.00	20.00	125.00
1,000,000	1905	3.00	6.00	12.00	100.00
1,700,000	1906	3.00	6.00	12.00	100.00
2,620,000	1907	1.50	4.00	8.00	90.00
776,666	1908	3.00	6.00	12.00	125.00
1,697,200 {	1909 with 1908 leaves	3.00	6.00	12.00	100.00
	1909 broad leaves	4.00	8.00	16.00	135.00
4,468,331	1910	1.50	3.00	6.50	50.00
	KING GEORGE V				
2,737,584	1911	8.00	12.50	25.00	200.00
3,235,557	1912	.75	1.25	3.00	50.00
3,613,937 {	1913 broad leaves	35.00	75.00	175.00	1000.00
	1913 (1914 leaves)	.75	1.25	3.00	50.00
2,549,811	1914	.75	1.25	3.00	50.00
688,057	1915	2.75	6.00	22.50	250.00
4,218,114	1916	.60	1.25	2.50	45.00
5,011,988	1917	.70	1.00	2.25	45.00
5,133,602	1918	.70	.80	2.00	45.00
7,877,722	1919	.70	.80	2.00	45.00
6,305,345	1920	.70	1.00	2.50	45.00
2,469,562	1921	.70	1.00	2.50	50.00
2,458,602	1928	.70	.80	2.00	45.00
3,253,888	1929	.70	.80	2.00	45.00

CANADIAN 10 CENTS SILVER (continued)

Quantity	Year	Very Good	Fine	Very Fine	Unc.
1,831,043	1930	$ .70	$1.00	$2.25	$45.00
2,067,421	1931	.70	.90	2.00	45.00
1,154,317	1932	.70	1.25	3.00	50.00
672,368	1933	1.00	2.50	5.00	60.00
409,067	1934	1.25	3.00	6.00	75.00
384,056	1935	2.00	5.00	10.00	175.00
2,460,871	1936	.70	1.50	2.00	30.00
192,194	1936 dot (outstanding rarity)				4000.00

KING GEORGE VI

Quantity	Year	Very Good	Fine	Very Fine	Unc.
2,499,138	1937	1.75	2.50	5.00	20.00
4,197,323	1938	.50	2.25	5.00	35.00
5,501,748	1939	.50	1.00	8.00	25.00
16,526,470	1940	.50	.70	1.00	9.50
8,716,386	1941	.50	.70	2.25	37.50
10,214,011	1942	.50	.70	1.00	20.00
21,143,229	1943	.50	.70	1.00	9.00
9,383,582	1944	.50	.70	1.00	9.00
10,979,570	1945	.50	.70	.75	7.50
6,300,066	1946		.70	.75	14.50
4,431,926	1947		.70	2.00	22.50
9,638,793	1947 ML		.70	.75	9.00
422,741	1948	4.50	7.50	11.50	55.00
11,120,006	1949			.70	4.50
17,823,595	1950			.70	4.50
15,079,265	1951			.70	4.50
10,476,340	1952			.70	3.75

QUEEN ELIZABETH II

Quantity	Year	Very Good	Fine	Very Fine	Unc.
18,467,020	1953			.25	3.25
4,435,795	1954			.75	7.00
12,294,649	1955			.25	2.25
16,732,844	1956			.30	4.50
15,631,952	1957				.75
10,908,306	1958				1.10
19,691,433	1959				.50
45,446,835	1960				.50
26,850,859	1961				.50
41,864,335	1962				.50
41,916.208	1963				.50
49,518,549	1964				.50
56,965,392	1965				.50
34,330,199	1966				.50
63,012,417	1967 mackerel reverse				.50
70,460,000	1968 .500 fine silver				.25
172,582,930	1968 pure nickel				.20
55,833,929	1969				.20
5,200,000	1970				.25
41,000,000	1971				.25
60,100,000	1972				.25
	1973				.25
	1974				.25
	1975				

Quantity	Year	Very Good	Fine	Very Fine	Unc.
750,000	1858	$40.00	$55.00	$75.00	$325.00

25 CENTS SILVER

The mint marks are below center of ribbon tying wreath on reverse.

QUEEN VICTORIA

900,000	1870	6.00	12.00	20.00	150.00
400,000	1871	10.00	16.00	25.00	250.00
748,000	1871 H	10.00	15.00	25.00	200.00
2,240,000	1872 H	2.00	4.00	10.00	150.00
1,600,000	1874 H	2.00	4.00	10.00	150.00
1,000,000	1875 H	95.00	200.00	400.00	1800.00
400,000 {	1880 H narrow "O"	11.50	16.50	30.00	260.00
	1880 H wide "O"	22.00	35.00	100.00	450.00
820,000	1881 H	6.00	12.00	25.00	200.00
600,000	1882 H	7.50	15.00	30.00	200.00
960,000	1883 H	3.50	7.00	20.00	175.00
192,000	1885	20.00	35.00	90.00	600.00
540,000	1886	6.00	12.00	25.00	250.00
100,000	1887	20.00	30.00	60.00	450.00
400,000	1888	6.00	12.00	25.00	175.00
66,324	1889	25.00	50.00	75.00	800.00
200,000	1890 H	7.00	14.00	25.00	250.00
120,000	1891	12.50	25.00	50.00	350.00
510,000	1892	4.00	9.00	18.00	175.00
100,000	1893	13.50	27.50	52.50	300.00
220,000	1894	6.00	12.00	20.00	225.00
415,580	1899	2.50	6.00	12.50	150.00
1,320,000	1900	2.00	4.50	10.00	125.00
640,000	1901	1.50	3.50	10.00	125.00

KING EDWARD VII

464,000	1902	3.00	6.00	14.00	125.00
800,000	1902 H	2.50	5.00	10.00	125.00
846,150	1903	3.00	6.00	15.00	155.00
400,000	1904	6.00	12.00	25.00	350.00
800,000	1905	3.00	6.00	15.00	200.00
1,237,843	1906	3.00	6.00	15.00	150.00
2,088,000	1907	3.00	6.00	15.00	150.00
495,016	1908	4.00	8.00	17.50	155.00
1,335,929	1909	2.50	4.00	10.00	200.00
3,577,569	1910	2.00	3.50	8.00	100.00

Quantity	Year	Very Good	Fine	Very Fine	Unc.

KING GEORGE V

Quantity	Year	Very Good	Fine	Very Fine	Unc.
1,721,341	1911	$9.00	$18.00	$42.50	$310.00
2,544,199	1912	1.00	2.50	7.00	90.00
2,213,595	1913	1.00	2.50	7.00	90.00
1,215,397	1914	1.50	3.00	8.00	110.00
242,382	1915	4.00	12.00	45.00	450.00
1,462,566	1916	1.50	3.00	6.00	65.00
3,365,644	1917	1.00	2.00	5.00	60.00
4,175,649	1918	1.00	2.00	5.00	60.00
5,852,262	1919	1.00	2.00	5.00	60.00
1,975,278	1920	1.25	2.50	6.00	75.00
597,337	1921	5.00	10.00	27.50	350.00
468,096	1927	10.00	20.00	50.00	400.00
2,114,178	1928	.75	1.50	4.00	50.00
2,690,562	1929	.75	1.50	4.00	50.00
968,748	1930	1.25	2.50	5.00	90.00
537,815	1931	1.50	3.50	7.00	150.00
537,994	1932	1.50	3.50	7.50	125.00
421,282	1933	1.75	4.00	8.00	90.00
384,350	1934	1.75	4.00	8.00	125.00
537,772	1935	1.35	3.50	7.00	110.00
972,094	1936	1.00	2.50	6.00	45.00
153,685	1936 dot	10.00	20.00	40.00	350.00

KING GEORGE VI

Quantity	Year	Very Good	Fine	Very Fine	Unc.
2,689,813	1937	1.50	3.00	4.00	17.50
3,149,245	1938	1.50	3.00	4.00	35.00
3,532,495	1939	1.50	3.00	4.00	25.00
9,583,650	1940	1.00	2.00	3.00	13.50
6,654,672	1941	1.00	2.00	3.00	12.50
6,935,871	1942	1.00	2.00	3.00	12.50
13,559,575	1943		1.50	2.00	12.50
7,216,237	1944		1.50	2.00	11.50
5,296,495	1945		1.50	2.00	10.00
2,210,810	1946		1.50	2.00	32.50
1,524,554	1947		1.50	3.00	55.00
4,393,938	1947 ML		2.00	3.00	10.00
2,564,424	1948			4.00	25.00
7,864,002	1949			2.00	7.00
9,673,335	1950			2.00	7.00
8,285,599	1951			1.25	6.00
8,861,657	1952			1.25	6.00

QUEEN ELIZABETH II

Quantity	Year	Unc.	Quantity	Year	Unc.
11,141,851	1953	$7.50	44,708,869	1965	$1.00
2,318,891	1954	35.00	25,388,892	1966	1.00
9,552,505	1955	10.00	48,863,764	1967 wildcat reverse	1.00
11,269,353	1956	7.00	71,500,000	1968 .500 silver	.75
12,364,001	1957	2.50	88,686,931	1968 pure nickel	.50
9,743,033	1958	2.50	133,037,929	1969	.50
13,503,461	1959	1.50	10,300,000	1970	.50
22,835,327	1960	1.00	48,100,000	1971	.50
18,164,368	1961	1.00		1972	.50
29,559,266	1962	1.00		1973 RCMP Comm.	.50
21,180,652	1963	1.00		1974	
36,479,343	1964	1.00		1975	

Quantity	Year	Very Good	Fine	Very Fine	Unc.

The mint marks are below center of ribbon tying wreath on reverse.

QUEEN VICTORIA

Quantity	Year	Very Good	Fine	Very Fine	Unc.
450,000	1870	$15.00	$25.00	$65.00	$500.00
200,000	1871	25.00	40.00	70.00	550.00
45,000	1871 H	40.00	65.00	150.00	700.00
80,000	1872 H	17.50	30.00	65.00	550.00
150,000	1881 H	17.50	30.00	60.00	600.00
60,000	1888	50.00	100.00	200.00	1000.00
20,000	1890 H	250.00	450.00	800.00	5000.00
151,000	1892	15.00	25.00	65.00	650.00
29,036	1894	65.00	140.00	325.00	2250.00
100,000	1898	17.50	27.50	60.00	550.00
50,000	1899	40.00	70.00	150.00	1000.00
118,000	1900	17.50	27.50	60.00	500.00
80,000	1901	17.50	27.50	60.00	500.00

KING EDWARD VII

Quantity	Year	Very Good	Fine	Very Fine	Unc.
120,000	1902	8.00	20.00	37.50	300.00
140,000	1903 H	10.00	22.50	45.00	450.00
60,000	1904	40.00	80.00	160.00	900.00
40,000	1905	25.00	55.00	110.00	850.00
350,000	1906	8.00	14.00	30.00	400.00
300,000	1907	8.00	14.00	30.00	400.00
128,119	1908	10.00	17.50	35.00	400.00
203,118	1909	7.00	12.50	35.00	450.00
649,521	1910	6.00	12.00	30.00	400.00

KING GEORGE V

Quantity	Year	Very Good	Fine	Very Fine	Unc.
209,972	1911	10.00	60.00	200.00	1000.00
285,867	1912	5.00	7.00	30.00	400.00
265,889	1913	5.00	7.00	30.00	400.00
160,128	1914	6.00	11.00	45.00	500.00
459,070	1916	4.00	6.00	18.00	300.00
752,213	1917	3.00	5.00	15.00	275.00
854,989	1918	3.00	5.00	15.00	275.00
1,113,429	1919	3.00	5.00	15.00	275.00
584,691	1920	3.00	5.00	15.00	275.00
206,398	1921 outstanding rarity	3500.00	5000.00	6000.00	9500.00
228,328	1929	4.00	5.00	10.00	250.00
57,581	1931	7.50	12.50	20.00	450.00
19,213	1932	35.00	50.00	110.00	800.00
39,539	1934	10.00	15.00	35.00	500.00
38,550	1936	10.00	15.00	35.00	300.00

KING GEORGE VI

Quantity	Year	Very Good	Fine	Very Fine	Unc.
192,016	1937		5.00	7.00	25.00
192,018	1938		6.00	15.00	175.00
287,976	1939		5.00	7.00	35.00
1,996,566	1940		4.00	5.00	15.00
1,974,165	1941		4.00	5.00	17.50
1,974,165	1942		4.00	5.00	16.50
3,109,583	1943		4.00	5.00	15.00
2,460,205	1944		4.00	5.00	15.00
1,959,528	1945		4.00	5.00	15.00
950,235	1946		4.00	5.00	35.00

Quantity	Year	Fine	Very Fine	Unc.
424,885 {	1947 straight 7........	$4.50	$5.50	$75.00
	1947 curved 7..........	4.00	5.00	70.00
38,433 {	1947 ML straight 7	30.00	35.00	125.00
	1947 ML curved 7	500.00	550.00	1250.00
37,784	1948......................	55.00	65.00	150.00
858,002	1949......................	3.50	4.50	15.00
2,384,179	1950......................	3.00	4.00	10.00
2,421,010	1951......................	3.00	4.00	8.50
2,598,337	1952......................	3.00	4.00	8.50

QUEEN ELIZABETH II

Quantity	Year	Unc.
1,781,191	1953......................	9.00
506,305	1954......................	22.00
753,511	1955......................	13.00
1,379,499	1956......................	6.50
2,171,689	1957......................	4.00
2,957,200	1958......................	3.50
3,095,535	1959......................	2.50
3,488,897	1960......................	1.50
3,584,417	1961......................	1.75
5,208,030	1962......................	1.75
8,348,871	1963......................	1.75
9,377,676	1964......................	1.75
12,629,974	1965......................	1.75
7,683,228	1966......................	1.75
4,221,135	1967 wolf reverse	4.25
3,966,932	1968 pure nickel (smaller planchet)	.75
7,113,929	1969......................	.75
2,400,000	1970......................	.75
2,160,000	1971......................	.75
	1972......................	.75
	1973......................	.75
	1974......................	.75
	1975......................	.75

Quantity	Year	Fine	Very Fine	Unc.

KING GEORGE V

428,707	1935	$15.00	$20.00	$55.00
306,100	1936	15.00	20.00	55.00

KING GEORGE VI

241,002	1937	15.00	20.00	50.00
90,304	1938	26.00	32.50	150.00

1,363,816	1939 Parliament buildings	6.00	8.50	25.00
38,391	1945	140.00	150.00	350.00
93,055	1946	25.00	35.00	90.00
65,595	1947 blunt 7	70.00	75.00	165.00
	1947 pointed 7	130.00	150.00	385.00
21,135	1947 ML	150.00	175.00	350.00
18,780	1948	400.00	450.00	800.00

Quantity	Year	Very Good	Fine	Very Fine	Unc.
641,840	1949 ship (New-foundland commem.)		$15.00	$22.50	$35.00
261,002	1950		9.00	11.00	30.00
411,395	1951		5.00	7.50	18.50
408,835	1952		5.00	7.50	18.50

QUEEN ELIZABETH II

Quantity	Year	Very Fine	Unc.
1,087,265	1953	5.00	9.00
242,815	1954	9.00	20.00
274,810	1955	9.00	20.00
209,092	1956	11.00	25.00
496,389	1957	5.00	9.00

Quantity	Year	Unc.
3,390,564	1958 Totem Pole (British Columbia Commem.)	8.00
1,443,502	1959	5.00
1,420,486	1960	5.00
1,262,231	1961	5.00
1,884,789	1962	4.00
4,179,981	1963	4.00
7,296,832	1964	4.00
10,768,569	1965	4.00
9,912,178	1966	4.00

Quantity	Year	Unc.

Quantity	Year	Unc.
6,694,571	1967 goose reverse.....................	$5.50
5,579,714	1968 pure nickel (smaller planchet)	1.50
4,809,313	1969	1.50
4,100,000	1970 (Manitoba Centennial)	1.75
	1971 (British Columbia Centennial) nickel	1.75
	1971 (British Columbia Centennial) silver	7.50
	1972 nickel	1.50
	1973 (Prince Edward Island Centennial) nickel	1.75
	1973 (Royal Canadian Mounted Police Centennial) silver	6.00

	Year	Unc.
	1974 (Winnipeg Centennial) nickel	1.75
	1974 (Winnipeg Centennial) silver	4.50
	1975 (Calgary Centennial) silver...	

QUEEN ELIZABETH II

CANADIAN SILVER 5 DOLLARS

1973 (Olympic Games Commemorative—
sailboats)............................... $8.50
1973 (Map of North America)......   8.50

CANADIAN SILVER 10 DOLLARS

1973 (Olympic Games Commemortive—
Montreal skyline) 17.50
1973 (Map of World)..................   17.50

The mint marks are above the date on the reverse.

Quantity	Year	Very Fine	Unc.
	KING EDWARD VII		
636	1908 C	$900.00	$1350.00
16,273	1909 C	100.00	150.00
28,012	1910 C	100.00	150.00
	KING GEORGE V		
256,946	1911 C	85.00	125.00
3,715	1913 C	650.00	1000.00
14,891	1914 C	150.00	275.00
6,111	1916 C	10,000.00	15,000.00
58,845	1917 C	85.00	125.00
106,516	1918 C	85.00	125.00
135,889	1919 C	85.00	125.00

5 DOLLARS GOLD

The mint marks are above the date on the reverse.

KING GEORGE V

165,680	1912	225.00	350.00
98,832	1913	225.00	350.00
31,122	1914	450.00	650.00

10 DOLLARS GOLD

The mint marks are above the date on the reverse.

KING GEORGE V

74,759	1912	350.00	725.00
149,232	1913	350.00	725.00
140,068	1914	375.00	750.00

20 DOLLARS GOLD

QUEEN ELIZABETH II

337,512	1967 (proof only)		150.00

9. GLOSSARY

Alloy A combination of gold or silver or copper with one or more other metals. The purpose is to produce a coin of more durable and cheaper composition.

Bullion Uncoined metal.

Commemorative coin A coin issued to honor an outstanding event or individual.

Condition The physical state of a coin—an important factor in determining its value.

Face value The denomination of a coin.

Incuse coin A coin on which the lettering and other details are sunk below the surface of the coin.

Mint mark A tiny letter struck on a coin to indicate the mint of origin.

Obverse The "head" of the coin—generally the side with the main design.

Overstrike The striking of new material or design on an already existing coin, hiding all or some of the original coin.

Pattern A trial piece which may or may not be issued for general use.

Premium value The price at which a collector can sell a coin (if above face value).

Reeded edge A coin edge with lines running across the thickness of the edge from obverse to reverse.

Reverse The "tail" of the coin—generally the side reserved for technical details, such as the denomination and date.

Types Classification of coins on the basis of the essential features of the design on the obverse. Examples: Indian Head Cent, Liberty Standing Half Dollar.

Value The market price of a coin (dealer's selling price) as contrasted to its face value.

INDEX